the 1998 dallas cowboys official team yearbook

THE HISTORY CHANNEL.

THE OFFICIAL NETWORK OF EVERY MILLENNIUM

WWW.HISTORYCHANNEL.COM

**Written and Edited by Dallas Cowboys
Public Relations Department**
Rich Dalrymple, Brett Daniels, Doug Hood and Rhonda Worthey

Photography by:
James Smith, Bill Kamenjar, Larry Torbett

Designers
Cami Marchitello
Kevin B. Scally

PUBLISHED BY

8055 West Manchester Blvd., Suite: # 455
Playa del Rey, CA 90293
Tel.: (310) 574-8161, Fax: (310) 448-4299
www.CWCSPORTS.com

CWC SPORTS, INC.

PRESIDENT
Lee Pfeifer

**SENIOR VICE-PRESIDENT
NEW BUSINESS DEVELOPMENT**
Mark Myden

VICE PRESIDENT-OPERATIONS
Louis Coulombe

**PUBLISHING ASSOCIATES
HECKMAN MEDIA, INC / SEATTLE**
Jim Heckman, President
Craig Olson, Vice President
SHERMAN MEDIA / CHICAGO
Harry Sherman, President
UNIVERSITY PUBLICATIONS / BOSTON
Steve Cadrain, President

SALES ASSOCIATES
John Garms / Detroit
Sam Colton / Chicago
Gulf Atlantic Industries / Scott Miller / Miami
Tom Myers / Dallas
University Sports Publications / New York

VICE PRESIDENT NATIONAL RETAIL SALES
Steeve Brassard

NATIONAL RETAIL SALES
Mike Landman

VICE PRESIDENT MEDIA SERVICES
Ray Raglin

PRODUCTION CONSULTANT
Patrick Parsons

ADMINISTRATIVE ASSISTANTS
Virginia Harrell
Sarka Jordankova

Special Thanks to:
Champion International Corp.
"The Paper Company"
Greg Burzell   John Hildenbiddle   Kenny Loyd

Table *of* Contents

TEXAS STADIUM

The glittering showcase of Cowboys Football is Texas Stadium, a state-of-the-art modern football facility which opened on October 24, 1971. Texas Stadium, located in the Dallas suburb of Irving, has a seating capacity of 65,675 and features two DiamondVision color replay screens, 381 luxury suites, 52 concession stands, 40 specialty stands, 86 restrooms, 115 drinking fountains and 130 acres of parking. Texas Stadium's most unique feature is the partial roof that covers fans from inclement weather, but leaves the game outdoors. In 1996, a new artificial turf surface was installed, making the playing field just another example of how Texas Stadium is constantly striving to remain one of the top football facilities in the United States.

The open air Corral, outside Gate 8, features food, beverage, entertainment and large screen televisions for fan hospitality before, during and after all Cowboys home games and special events. New for 1998 at Texas Stadium are three themed sports bars located on the lower concourse level.

Tours of Texas Stadium are available every hour on the hour Monday through Sunday, when no events are scheduled. Tickets are $5.00 for adults and $3.00 for children. Tours originate at the Cowboys souvenir shop, The Pro Shop, which is open daily on the grounds outside the stadium at Gate 8. For more information on Pro Shop merchandise and tours, call 972-554-1804.

For information on Texas Stadium Suite sales and leasing, call 972-556-9396. For information on hosting a banquet or catering an event at the stadium call 972-554-6368.

COWBOYS TICKETS

Order by phone, mail, or in person. Season tickets and group ticket sales are available by calling the Cowboys Ticket Office at 972-579-4800. Individual game tickets are available by calling Ticketmaster Phone Centers (214/373-8000) or at Ticketmaster outlets including Foley's, Fiesta and Tom Thumb. Convenience charges are added at Ticketmaster locations and are non-refundable. Ticket prices are $55, $50, $35 and $34 each.

COWBOYS ON TV

All Cowboys games are televised. Regular season games are carried by the national networks — FOX, ABC, CBS or ESPN. Check your local listings for times and stations. Preseason games that are not carried by a network, will be broadcast by KDFW-TV, Channel 4 in Dallas/Ft. Worth.

The "Chan Gailey Show" is televised by KDFW, Channel 4 (Dallas-Ft. Worth), every Sunday morning during the season at 10:30 a.m. It is also shown on the regionally syndicated SilverStar network to nearly 30 regional stations. Check your local listings.

"Cowboys Special Edition," featuring Jerry Jones, is a magazine-style inside look at the team that is televised by KDFW, Channel 4 (Dallas-Ft. Worth) every Sunday morning at 9:30 a.m. during the season. This program is also syndicated regionally across the SilverStar Network. Check your local listings for broadcast times in your area.

For every deadline, a finish line.

In business, you don't always have to come in first to win. You just have to come up with the right solution at the right time. That's why UPS offers a whole range of guaranteed, on-time delivery options.* More than anyone else, in fact. It's part of our commitment to meeting the demands of your business. And a good example of why when it comes to helping you be more competitive, there's really no competition.

MOVING at the SPEED of BUSINESS.

www.ups.com · 1-800-PICK-UPS

Official Package
Delivery Company

On sharp curves, even the car smiles.

For more information, call 1-800-334-4BMW.
Internet address: http://www.bmwusa.com

BMWs are engineered to do things other cars can't. Which tends to put a pretty big smile on their owners' faces. And so does standard All Season Traction and standard Scheduled Maintenance for 3 years/36,000 miles. For a permanent grin, see your local authorized BMW center for a test drive.

The Ultimate Driving Machine®

Richardson
Classic BMW
300 N. Central Expressway
Exit 25
972-918-1100

Dallas
John Roberts BMW
2536 Forest Lane
972-247-7233

Arlington
Moritz BMW
2001 N. Collins Street
817-461-9222

Fort Worth
Autobahn Motorcars
2828 White Settlement Road
817-336-0885

COWBOYS ON RADIO

KVIL-FM, 103.7 enters its eighth year of originating the Cowboys' game broadcasts. Returning to the Dallas broadcast booth for his 20th season will be play-by-play man Brad Sham. Babe Laufenberg (color analysis) will join Sham in bringing all the action and excitement to listeners across the country.

KVIL's creative approach to pre-game coverage begins two hours prior to each kickoff. Live post-game locker room interviews with players and coaches will follow each game.

Cowboys games are also broadcast in Spanish on the "Dallas Cowboys Radio Network in Spanish" to stations throughout Texas, the southwest and Mexico.

COWBOYS IN PRINT

"The Dallas Cowboys Weekly" is the biggest and best team publication in sports. Thirty-two issues a year bring you comprehensive game coverage, great color photography, player and cheerleader profiles and much more. Call now for a 32-week subscription ($35.00) at 972-556-9972.

"Cowboys Insider" is the souvenir magazine sold only at Cowboys home games. "Cowboys Insider" gives you lineups, player photos, updated statistics, feature stories from around the NFL and inside information on the Cowboys' opponent.

COWBOYS ON THE INTERNET

The Dallas Cowboys homepage can be found at www.dallascowboys.com . It is the most comprehensive spot on the internet for up to date information on the Dallas Cowboys and the Dallas Cowboys Cheerleaders. Updated daily with schedules, press releases, statistics and player bios, the Cowboys homepage is a must-see for anyone with a computer. You can also see and order the latest Cowboys merchandise through The Pro Shop at www.dallascowboys.com.

COWBOYS VIDEOTAPES

You can order annual Cowboys highlight tapes, including the Cowboys 1997 film entitled "Bright Future, Proud Past" along with Super Bowl films and video team histories from the video library of award-winning NFL Films. Call toll-free 1-800-NFL-GIFT.

DALLAS COWBOYS 1998 SCHEDULE

DATE	PRESEASON GAMES (TV)	(Dallas Time) KICKOFF
Fri., July 31	SEATTLE (Ch. 4, Dallas)	8:00 P.M.
Sat., Aug. 8	OAKLAND (Ch. 4, Dallas)	8:00 P.M.
Mon., Aug. 17	NEW ENGLAND @ Mexico City (ABC)*	7:00 P.M.
Sat., Aug. 22	@ St. Louis (Ch.4, Dallas)	7:00 P.M.
Thur., Aug. 27	@ Jacksonville (CBS)*	7:00 P.M.
REGULAR-SEASON	GAMES (TV)	
Sun., Sept. 6	ARIZONA (FOX)	3:05 P.M.
Sun., Sept. 13	@ Denver (FOX)	3:15 P.M.
Mon., Sept. 21	@ New York Giants (ABC)*	7:20 P.M.
Sun., Sept. 27	OAKLAND (CBS)	12:01 P.M.
Sun., Oct. 4	@ Washington (FOX)	12:01 P.M.
Sun., Oct. 11	CAROLINA (FOX)	12:01 P.M.
Sun., Oct. 18	@ Chicago (FOX)	3:15 P.M.
Sun., Oct. 25	Bye	
Mon., Nov. 2	@ Philadelphia (ABC)*	7:20 P.M.
Sun., Nov. 8	NEW YORK GIANTS (FOX)	12:01 P.M.
Sun., Nov. 15	@ Arizona (FOX)	3:15 P.M.
Sun., Nov. 22	SEATTLE (CBS)	12:01 P.M.
Thurs., Nov. 26	MINNESOTA (FOX)*	3:05 P.M.
Sun., Dec. 6	@ New Orleans (FOX)	12:01 P.M.
Sun., Dec. 13	@ Kansas City (FOX)	3:15 P.M.
Sun., Dec. 20	PHILADELPHIA (FOX)	3:15 P.M.
Sun., Dec. 27	WASHINGTON (ESPN)*	7:20 P.M.

*Televised Nationally

WILD CARD WEEKEND	Jan. 2-3, 1999
DIVISIONAL PLAYOFFS	Jan. 9-10, 1999
CONFERENCE CHAMPIONSHIPS	Jan. 17, 1999
SUPER BOWL XXXIII (Miami, FL)	Jan. 31, 1999
PRO BOWL (Honolulu, HI)	Feb. 7, 1999

At the time of Jerry Jones' purchase of the Dallas Cowboys in 1989, the proud franchise was struggling through the most difficult period in club history.

For the first time since 1964, the Cowboys had posted losing seasons for three consecutive years, and the club had closed the 1988 season with the worst record in the NFL.

In the ensuing years of Jones' ownership, fans of the Dallas Cowboys witnessed what might have been the most dramatic and visible turnaround in the history of professional sports. A team that closed the 1980s with a pair of seasons that netted just four wins would take hold of the 1990s with three Super Bowl titles, four straight NFC Championship Game appearances and an unprecedented five straight NFC Eastern Division crowns.

Jones' immediate vision was to put a championship team on the field, while also restoring the pride of a fan following that spans the nation and reaches all corners of the world. In a matter of months, that vision became reality. By January of 1993, the Cowboys earned a Super Bowl championship for the first time in 15 seasons, and the following year, the Cowboys became the fifth team to win back-to-back Super Bowl crowns.

In 1995, the Dallas Cowboys became the first NFL franchise to win three Super Bowls in a four year period of time, while tying the NFL record for the most Super Bowl victories by an organization with five. In 1996, the club claimed its fifth straight division title, a feat that had never been reached before by any NFC Eastern Division team.

Along the way, Jones established himself as one of the NFL's most influential and active owners. His "hands on" leadership ability has played a prominent role in the resurgence of the Cowboys, and his contributions to the National Football League have been prominent and productive.

★ In the last 19 years, 18 different owners have entered the National Football League. Of that group, only Jerry Jones has guided his franchise to more than one Super Bowl championship. Moreover, Jones joins Art Rooney, Jack Kent Cooke, Al Davis and Eddie DeBartolo as the only men to own NFL franchises that have won at least three Super Bowls.

★ The fan following and interest in the current era of the Cowboys has reached unprecedented levels in the national and international spotlight. At the end of the

Jerry Jones
Owner/General Manager

1997 season, the team had played before 129 straight sold out stadiums (home and away). In addition, Dallas' three most recent Super Bowl appearances represent the three most watched television programs in history.

★ As a member of the league's Broadcasting Committee, Jones was a key player in the agreement that introduced the FOX Network to the NFL as the rights holder for the NFC television package in 1993. In addition, he was a prominent voice in the most recent NFL television agreement that set the standard for all of professional sports in terms of network television partnerships.

★ With his appointment to the NFL's prestigious Competition Committee in May of 1992, Jones became the first owner to serve in that capacity since the late Paul Brown. He has since moved to the Executive Committee of the NFL's Management Council.

★ During the club's run to the 1992 World Championship, the Cowboys set a team record for most wins in a regular season (13) and most overall wins (16). Following

the 1995 season, the Cowboys appeared in a NFL-record eighth Super Bowl. The Cowboys are now the only team in the NFL that has won multiple Super Bowl titles in two separate decades.

★ After the inaugural 1-15 season in 1989, Jones was the NFL's most aggressive executive in the area of Plan B free agency — signing 16 Plan B players. Three of those players went on to start in Super Bowl XXVII, and tight end Jay Novacek was selected to five Pro Bowls.

★ Within a two year period, Jones signed five players to the most lucrative contracts ever paid for individual players at their respective positions at the time of their signings. Between September of 1993 and September of 1995, Cowboys running back Emmitt Smith, quarterback Troy Aikman, fullback Daryl Johnston, wide receiver Michael Irvin and cornerback Deion Sanders all signed contracts that made them the highest paid NFL players to ever play their position.

★ In May of 1997, *Financial World* magazine recognized Jones as the owner of the most valuable sports team in all of professional athletics. The Cowboys carried that "most valuable franchise" tag throughout 1993, 1994, 1995 and 1996.

★ In November of 1994, Jones was selected as the Master Entrepreneur of the Year by Ernst and Young and *Inc.* magazine. In December of 1994, he was named one of America's 10 Most Interesting People in a nationally televised Barbara Walters special on ABC.

★ In the summer of 1991, Jones was voted as the best sports franchise owner in the Dallas-Ft. Worth metroplex, receiving 48% of the votes that were tabulated in a Dallas Morning News readers' poll. Four years later, a Fort Worth Star Telegram readers' poll recognized Jones with the same distinction.

★ In February of 1992, Jones was named the winner of the "Big D Award" by the Dallas All Sports Association. The "Big D Award" annually recognizes the sports figure who has done the most to bring excitement to the Metroplex through athletics. More recently, Jones was ranked 23rd in *The Sporting News'* list of the 100 Most Powerful People in Sports for 1997.

Jerral Wayne Jones was born on Oct. 13, 1942 in Los Angeles. He learned his business style from his father, J.W. "Pat" Jones, a

This is not an Independent Insurance Agent...
...It's your most important Business Partner

In today's complex world of insurance, you need a proven professional who can help you compete. Your Independent Insurance Agent knows the insurance needs of your business, and your community. Put them to work for you and take advantage of their years of experience. If you do, you'll realize what we at Travelers have known for over 130 years. The Independent Insurance Agent is your most valuable business partner.

We've made choosing the right business partner easier.
Call your local Travelers Agent today.

successful entrepreneur first in supermarkets, then in insurance.

Pat Jones moved his family to North Little Rock, Ark., soon after Jerry was born. After starring as a running back at North Little Rock High School, Jerry received a scholarship to play football at the University of Arkansas. He was a starting guard and co-captain of the 1964 team that went 11-0, defeated Nebraska in the Cotton Bowl and captured the national championship.

Upon graduating with a M.B.A. from Arkansas in 1965, Jerry joined his father's insurance company, Modern Security Life in Springfield, Mo., as executive vice president.

Jones entered the oil and gas exploration business in Oklahoma in 1970 and soon became a phenomenal success. His oil and gas concern now has offices in Fort Smith, Ark., and Calgary, Canada.

One of a very small number of NFL owners who actually earned a significant level of success as a football player, Jones is currently living his dream of engineering the fortunes of a NFL franchise. A man of varied interests who will not rest on yesterday's achievements, he is a dedicated businessman and family man—sharing a passion for both worlds.

Jerry is also involved in numerous civic and charitable causes. As very strong supporters of the Salvation Army, Jerry and his wife Gene were recently presented the Army's Partner of the Year Award on behalf of the Cowboys organization. The Jones family is also very actively involved with several other community related organizations, including the Children's Medical Center of Dallas, the National Board for the Boys and Girls Clubs of America and the Kent Waldrep Paralysis Foundation.

Jerry and wife Gene, a former Arkansas beauty pageant winner whom he met while both attended the University of Arkansas, live in Dallas. They have three children, Stephen, Charlotte and Jerry, Jr., and five grandchildren.

Stephen (6/21/64) is a graduate of the University of Arkansas who serves as the Cowboys' Vice President/Director of Player Personnel, and Charlotte (7/26/66) is a Stanford graduate who is the Cowboys Vice President/Director of Marketing and Special Events. Jerry Jr. (9/27/69), a graduate of Georgetown University who earned his law degree from Southern Methodist University, is the Cowboys' Vice President for Legal Operations.

Chronology Since Jerry Jones' Purchase of the Dallas Cowboys

February 25, 1989 - Jones purchases the Dallas Cowboys and the lease to manage Texas Stadium Corp. from H.R. "Bum" Bright. Jerry Jones names Jimmy Johnson as the new head coach of the Dallas Cowboys.

October 12, 1989 - Herschel Walker is traded to Minnesota for five players, six conditional draft choices, and a 1992 first round draft choice. Current players who actually came to Dallas as a result of the trade include: Emmitt Smith, Kevin Smith and Darren Woodson.

September 29, 1991 - Dallas defeats the defending Super Bowl Champion New York Giants by a 21-16 score at Texas Stadium.

November 24, 1991 - The Cowboys end the Washington Redskins' 1991 undefeated streak at 11 games with a 24-21 victory at RFK.

December 15, 1991 - Dallas defeats Philadelphia, 25-13, at Veterans Stadium to secure a wild card playoff spot. The victory marks the team's first trip to the playoffs since the 1985 club went 10-6 and won the NFC Eastern Division title.

December 22, 1991 - Dallas closes the 1991 season with a 31-27 win over Atlanta, marking the team's best record (11-5) since the 1983 team finished 12-4.

January 5, 1992 - Dallas defeats Chicago by a 17-13 score in an opening round playoff game at Soldier Field. The victory marks the Cowboys' first playoff win since 1982, and the first playoff win on the road since 1980.

December 21, 1992 - Before a national television audience on ABC's Monday Night Football, the Cowboys defeat the Atlanta Falcons (41-17) at the Georgia Dome to claim the NFC Eastern Division Championship. The victory marks the Cowboys' first divisional title since 1985. It is the 14th divisional title in club history.

December 27, 1992 - Dallas defeats Chicago by a 27-14 score at Texas Stadium. The victory is the 13th of the year for Dallas, establishing a new club record for victories in a season. In the Bears game, Emmitt Smith finishes the season with 1,713 rushing yards,

enabling him to become the first player to win back-to-back NFL rushing titles since Eric Dickerson (1983-84).

January 17, 1993 - In their first NFC Championship Game since 1982, the Cowboys defeat the San Francisco 49ers by a 30-20 score at Candlestick Park. The victory sends Dallas to Super Bowl XXVII in Pasadena, marking the Cowboys first Super Bowl trip since 1978.

January 31, 1993 - While making a NFL record sixth Super Bowl appearance, the Cowboys defeat Buffalo 52-17 in Super Bowl XXVII at the Rose Bowl in Pasadena. The victory enables the Cowboys to become the only franchise in NFL history to win more than one Super Bowl under two different ownerships. Troy Aikman was named the game's MVP after throwing four touchdown passes.

January 2, 1994 - The Cowboys defeat the New York Giants 16-13 in overtime at the Meadowlands. The victory clinches the Cowboys' second straight NFC East title and the 15th division crown in club history.

January 2, 1994 - Emmitt Smith finishes the season with 1,486 yards to earn his third straight NFL rushing crown. He becomes just the fourth man in NFL history to win three consecutive rushing titles.

January 23, 1994 - Dallas defeats San Francisco 38-21 in the NFC Championship Game at Texas Stadium. The victory gives the Cowboys a NFL-record seventh conference championship in the first conference title game to be played at Texas Stadium since Jan. 1, 1978 (a 23-6 win over Minnesota).

January 30, 1994 - Dallas becomes one of just three NFL teams to win four Super Bowls

by defeating Buffalo (30-13) in Super Bowl XXVIII. The game, played at the Georgia Dome in Atlanta, featured two rushing touchdown's by Super Bowl MVP Emmitt Smith. Dallas raised its NFL record number of Super Bowl appearances to seven.

March 30, 1994 - Barry Switzer is named the new head coach of the Dallas Cowboys - and the third head coach in team history. Switzer replaces Jimmy Johnson who stepped down as the Cowboys' head coach the previous day.

January 15, 1995 - The Cowboys play in their third NFC Championship Game of the decade. The Cowboys are the only NFL team to play in multiple conference championship games in each decade of the team's existence.

December 25, 1995 - Emmitt Smith closes the season with a team record 1,773 rushing yards and a NFL record 25 touchdowns. Smith led the NFL in rushing for the fourth time in five years, becoming just the fifth player in NFL history to win at least four rushing titles.

January 14, 1996 - The Cowboys win a NFL record eighth conference championship game by defeating the Green Bay Packers 38-27 at Texas Stadium. The victory marked the Cowboys third NFC title in four years and ensured the team of a NFL-record eighth Super Bowl appearance.

January 28, 1996 - Dallas becomes the first team in NFL history to win three Super Bowls in a four-year period by defeating the Pittsburgh Steelers 27-17 in Super Bowl XXX at Sun Devil Stadium in Tempe, Arizona. The game is witnessed by 138.4 million television viewers, making Super Bowl XXX the most

watched event in television history. The victory enables Dallas to earn its fifth Super Bowl title - joining the San Francisco 49ers as the only NFL franchises to win five Super Bowls.

December 15, 1996 - The Cowboys clinch a fifth straight division title with a 12-6 win over the New England Patriots at Texas Stadium. The championship enables the Cowboys to become the first team in NFL history to win five straight NFC Eastern Division crowns.

December, 1997 - The Cowboys close the 1997 season with a 6-10 record, marking the team's first non-playoff season since 1990. The team played before 16 straight sold-out regular season games in 1997, bringing the club's NFL record streak to 129 straight sold out games (home or away). The streak, which includes playoff games, dates back to December 16, 1990 - vs. Phoenix - at Texas Stadium (the last non-sell-out). The Cowboys season-ending loss to the New York Giants (12/21/97) marked the 63rd straight sell-out at Texas Stadium (including playoffs), while the final road game of the season at Cincinnati (12/14/97) marked the 64th straight sell-out for the Cowboys away from home (including playoffs).

February 12, 1998 - Jerry Jones names Chan Gailey as the fourth head coach in the history of the Dallas Cowboys franchise. Gailey, who had previously served as the Pittsburgh Steelers offensive coordinator, replaces Barry Switzer, who resigned from his position on January 9th.

COWBOYS

Go Long!

The Ericsson Digital PCS lineup.

The Ericsson LX 677, LX 700 and LX 788* work almost anywhere you go. And with the new AT&T Digital One Rate℠, you get the same low rate no matter where you are. So every call is like a local call. Plus, these phones are packed with the features you want most, like voice mail, short message service and incredibly long talk and standby times.

Check out these Ericsson Digital PCS phones and AT&T Digital One Rate today.
Whether you're home or away, it's never been easier to stay in touch.

AT&T Wireless Services

For more information, call
1 800-IMAGINE®

Stephen Jones
Executive VP/Director of Player Personnel

With just under ten years worth of NFL experience under his belt, Stephen Jones' reputation as one of the brightest young executives in professional sports continues to grow. Named a Cowboys Vice President in February of 1989, Jones coordinates the Cowboys' entire player personnel department. He also oversees the negotiation of all player contracts, management of the salary cap, the operation of Texas Stadium and a wide range of other club related duties.

In the ever-evolving role of the salary cap in the current collective bargaining agreement, Jones' performance in managing the Cowboys player payroll has played a prominent role in the teams' ability to compete at the NFL's highest level.

Jones' involvement in shaping the Dallas roster under the salary cap has been critical in allowing the Cowboys to maintain one of the NFL's most talented core group of players throughout the decade of the 1990s.

During a historic two-year period of time, Jones was involved in signing five Cowboys stars to the most lucrative contracts ever paid for individual players at their respective positions. Between September of 1993 and September of 1995, Jones helped orchestrate contract agreements that made Cowboys running back Emmitt Smith, quarterback Troy Aikman, fullback Daryl Johnston, wide receiver Michael Irvin and cornerback Deion Sanders the highest paid NFL players to ever play their positions at the time of their signing.

Entering his 10th year as a NFL executive, Jones has enjoyed a life-long association with the game of football. A four-year letterman as a linebacker and special teams standout at the University of Arkansas, Jones was a starter for the Razorbacks in the Orange Bowl Classic Game that followed the 1986 season.

Prior to attending the University of Arkansas, Jones was also an all-state quarterback and a three-year starter at Catholic High School in Little Rock.

He graduated from Arkansas in 1988 with a degree in chemical engineering and went to work in the oil and gas business for JMC Exploration as an engineer.

On Feb. 25, 1989, Jerry Jones purchased the Dallas Cowboys and installed Stephen into a key front office position as one of three vice presidents with the club.

Jones is actively involved with the Young Presidents Organization. He also serves on the board of directors for the Kent Waldrep National Paralysis Foundation and the G.T.E./S.M.U Athletic Forum.

Jones (6/21/64) was born and raised in Little Rock. He is married to the former Karen Hickman of El Dorado, Arkansas, and the couple has three daughters: Jessica(8/24/92), Jordan (10/8/93) and Caroline(4/4/97).

LARRY LACEWELL
Director of College and Pro Scouting

Larry Lacewell joined the Cowboys as Director of College Scouting in May of 1992, and he has coordinated the Cowboys' NFL Draft efforts from 1993 to 1998. In the spring of 1994, he was charged with the additional responsibility of overseeing pro personnel. Lacewell now directs the Cowboys personnel evaluation for all college prospects, as well as the NFL's 29 other teams.

In 1997, the Cowboys enjoyed a very productive draft as all nine of the team's selections stayed with the club throughout the entire season. The class was highlighted by third-round choice Dexter Coakley, who started all 16 games at outside linebacker and earned All-Rookie recognition from the Pro Football Writers of America and *Pro Football Weekly*. First-round pick, tight end David LaFleur, also had a strong showing as a rookie, catching 18 passes for 122 yards. Seventh-round safety Omar Stoutmire tied for the team lead with two interceptions and was seventh among NFL rookies with 76 tackles.

In 1996, seven of the nine players the Cowboys drafted went on to earn a roster spot. That class was highlighted by second-round selection Randall Godfrey, who earned a starting linebacker's position by mid-November on a defensive unit that finished the year ranked third in the NFL.

In 1994, six of Dallas' seven draftees earned roster spots, and second-round offensive tackle Larry Allen, who is considered one of the NFL's finest young offensive lineman, earned a Pro Bowl selection as a second year player in 1995.

Lacewell joined the NFL ranks with the Cowboys after a distinguished career in collegiate coaching and athletic administration that spanned over 30 years.

Lacewell served under Johnny Majors as the defensive coordinator at Tennessee (1990-1991). As the athletic director and head coach at Arkansas State (1978-89), Lacewell compiled a record of 69-48-4. He was named the Southland Conference's Coach of the Year on three occasions, while the Indians captured two conference titles under his direction.

Lacewell began his coaching career as an assistant at Alabama in 1959. Following two seasons with the Crimson Tide, he moved on to Arkansas State (1961), Arkansas A&M (1962-63), Kilgore Junior College (1964-65), Oklahoma (1966), Wichita State (1967) and Iowa State (1968). Lacewell rejoined the Sooners' staff in 1969 as assistant head coach and defensive coordinator, and over the next nine seasons helped Oklahoma to six Big Eight titles and two national championships.

A native of Fordyce, AR, Lacewell (2/12/37) attended Fordyce High School and then played halfback at Arkansas A&M from 1955-59. In 1996, Lacewell was inducted into the Arkansas Sports Hall of Fame. He and his wife Criss have two sons, Bryant Land and Logan.

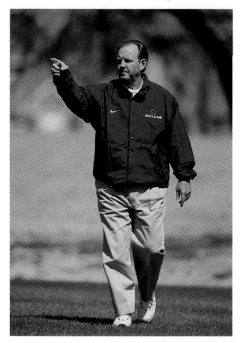

Chan Gailey
Head Coach
College: Florida
NFL: 11th season
Cowboys: 1st season

Success has been a companion of Chan Gailey's at every stop along his coaching career. With each challenge and opportunity, Gailey has displayed the character, consistency and performance of a winner. Those qualities, and a reputation for being one of the NFL's brightest and most innovative coaching minds, enabled Gailey to land in Texas as Jerry Jones' selection to become the fourth head coach in the 39 year history of the Dallas Cowboys.

On February 12, 1998, Jones introduced Thomas Chandler Gailey to the players, fans and followers of the Dallas Cowboys, and a new era in the storied history of the NFL's most widely followed franchise was underway.

Gailey's rise to prominence in the NFL was built upon a solid reputation as one of the league's most creative and productive offensive coaches. Gailey is also noted for being a consistent winner. In 10 seasons as an assistant coach in the NFL, he has appeared in four Super Bowls, six AFC Championship Games and helped his teams win seven division titles. In eight of the ten seasons he has been a NFL assistant, he has been with a team that has had 10-or-more wins. In ten seasons in the NFL, Gailey's teams have been on the winning side of the field for exactly 100 regular season victories.

In addition to his accomplishments as a NFL assistant, Gailey has earned respect from his peers and proven himself as a productive head coach.

In five seasons as a head coach, two years in the World League and three years in

college, Gailey has posted a 36-18-1 record, good for a .664 winning percentage. In addition, he reached postseason play three times, capturing the NCAA Division II Championship at Troy State University in 1984.

As an assistant with Pittsburgh (1994-97), Gailey was instrumental in developing the young offensive talent that helped the Steelers capture four consecutive AFC Central Division titles and appear in three of the last four AFC Championship Games, including an AFC title and Super Bowl XXX appearance following the 1995 season. While free agency stripped the Steelers of Pro Bowl tight end Eric Green and guard Duval Love, as well as quarterback Neil O'Donnell, tackle Leon Searcy and wide receiver Andre Hastings — the team's leading receiver in 1996 — Gailey continued to plug in new players and keep the ball moving.

In two years as the Pittsburgh offensive coordinator, Gailey created one the NFL's most potent running attacks. The 1997 Steelers led the NFL in rushing, rolling up 154.9 yards-per-game on the ground. That figure topped the 143.7 yards-per-game his 1996 offense produced on the ground, which was second in the NFL and the best output by a Pittsburgh running game since 1983. Running back Jerome Bettis finished the 1997 season as the NFL's third leading rusher with a career-high 1,665 yards and a 4.4 yard-per-carry average. That followed a 1996 season in which he rushed for 1,431 yards and 11 touchdowns.

Gailey's understanding of the professional passing game, and his ability to develop quarterbacks were also evident during his time in Pittsburgh. Teams were unable to load up against the run when facing the Steelers in 1997 because of the rapid development of quarterback Kordell Stewart. A first-year starter in 1997, Stewart threw for 3,020 yards and 21 touchdowns, the most touchdown passes by a Steelers' quarterback since Terry Bradshaw threw 22 in 1981. Stewart led the Steelers to within one game of Super Bowl XXXII, while Mike Tomzcak guided Pittsburgh to

an 11-5 playoff season under Gailey's offensive direction in 1996.

During his first two seasons in Pittsburgh (1994-95), Gailey served as the team's wide receivers coach. His star pupil was Yancey Thigpen, a player who entered the 1994 season with 10 career receptions in his first three years in the NFL. Thigpen showed his potential in 1994 when he recorded 36 catches for 546 yards and four touchdowns. The 1995 season, his second under Gailey, was his breakout year. On his way to Pro Bowl honors, Thigpen recorded a club-record 85 receptions for 1,307 yards and five touchdowns. During that 1995 season, Gailey was also instrumental in the creation of the "Slash" offensive package featuring rookie Kordell Stewart.

Gailey's other NFL experience came during a six-year stint (1985-90) as an assistant under former Dallas Cowboys' running back Dan Reeves at Denver. In his first season with the Broncos, Gailey served as a defensive assistant and special teams coach. The following year, he moved to the offensive side of the ball, coaching the special teams and tight ends. Working under offensive coordinator Mike Shanahan, Gailey and the Broncos captured the AFC title and a berth in Super Bowl XXI. In 1987, he was in charge of the tight ends and wide receivers, overseeing The Three Amigos (Vance Johnson, Ricky Nattiel,

Mark Jackson). Gailey took over the quarterback coaching duties in 1988 following the departure of Shanahan to the Raiders as head coach.

The 1989 season was Gailey's first as the Broncos offensive coordinator. The Broncos posted an 11-5 record, captured the AFC title, and earned a berth in Super Bowl XXIV behind his offense. That squad finished sixth in the NFL in rushing behind rookie running back Bobby Humphrey, who ran for 1,151 yards. John Elway threw for 3,051 yards and 18 touchdowns in providing Denver a balanced attack. The 1990 offense saw Elway's passing numbers jump to 3,526 yards and Humphrey's rushing totals reach 1,202 yards.

The 1989-90 Broncos coaching staff featured Dan Reeves (Head Coach), Chan Gailey (Offensive Coordinator), Wade Phillips (Defensive Coordinator) and Mike Shanahan (Quarterbacks). Reeves, Phillips and Shanahan have all guided teams to the playoffs as head coaches, including four Super Bowl appearances.

Sandwiched between his two NFL tours of duty, were head coaching stops in the World League with the Birmingham Fire (1991-92) and at Samford University (1993). While with the Fire, Gailey produced back-to-back playoff appearances while posting 5-5 and 7-2-1 records. Gailey is the first former World League (now NFL Europe) head coach to become a NFL head coach. In his one year at Samford, the Bulldogs went 5-6.

Gailey began his coaching career as a graduate assistant at his alma mater Florida from 1974-75. He then moved on to Troy State University, where he served as the secondary coach from 1976-78. That was followed by four years under Ken Hatfield at the Air Force Academy (1979-82), serving as a defensive assistant the first two seasons and the defensive coordinator his last two seasons.

Gailey returned to Troy State as head coach for the 1983-84 seasons. His 1984 team won the NCAA Division II National Championship, and he was honored as conference coach of the year. He joined the Denver Broncos following his championship season.

Chan Gailey was born on January 5, 1952 in Gainesville, Georgia. While growing up in Americus, Georgia, his Little League baseball coach was former Cowboys running back and current Atlanta Falcons head coach Dan Reeves. Gailey followed Reeves as a multi-sport star at Americus High School before attending the University of Florida on a football scholarship. Gailey was a three-year letterman at quarterback for the Gators (1971-73), and he graduated from Florida in 1974 with a degree in physical education.

Chan and his wife Laurie, a native of Americus, Ga., have two sons, Tate (21) and Andrew (17).

What they are saying about Chan Gailey:

"The Steeler organization is very happy for Chan Gailey. He's done a great job here in Pittsburgh not only with our receivers, but also with the development of Kordell Stewart and our entire offense."
Pittsburgh Steelers Director of Football Operations Tom Donahoe

"I think Dallas is getting a very good coach and someone who is going to be an excellent head coach. We are going to miss him greatly. Not only are they getting a solid football coach, but they are also getting a very good person. In this day and age, I don't think you can ever minimize the importance of adding good people to your organization. Chan Gailey will give Dallas every opportunity to be successful."
Pittsburgh Steelers Head Football Coach Bill Cowher

"I think the Cowboys are going to be very delighted with Chan. He is a great coach and a quality person. Troy is going to enjoy working with him as I did during his days here in Denver. I am very happy for Chan and his opportunity, and I think you are going to see that he is going to be one of the great coaches in this league."
Denver Broncos Quarterback John Elway

"The Cowboys couldn't have picked a better guy. Chan Gailey is the perfect man for the job."
Denver Broncos Head Coach Mike Shanahan

"I've known Chan since he was little. We grew up together in Americus, and I have followed his career ever since. I can't think of one single thing bad to say about Chan, and I don't think anyone who has been associated with Chan can either. He has always been a great athlete and a great competitor. He has proven he is a good football coach at every level of the game. He has been a special teams coach, a defensive coordinator and an offensive coordinator. I brought him into the NFL in 1985 because he had a tremendous background in football, and I think he is ready to be a head coach."
Atlanta Falcons Head Coach Dan Reeves

"With Chan in Pittsburgh, they did an outstanding job of utilizing all of their personnel. The development of Kordell Stewart as an outstanding young quarterback in the NFL is a tribute to Kordell's talent, but it is also a tribute to the designs and work of the Pittsburgh staff and especially Chan Gailey. The structure and style of their attack was extensive, they were diversified with multiple formations, and you could count on seeing one or two gadget plays. Chan runs a diversified offense with good ideas and good schemes."
Jacksonville Jaguars Head Coach Tom Coughlin

CHAN GAILEY
COACHING HISTORY

Year – Location	Record	Achievements
1974 – University of Florida (Graduate Assistant)	8-4	Lost Sugar Bowl
1975 – University of Florida (Graduate Assistant)	9-3	Lost Gator Bowl
1976 – Troy State University (Secondary)	8-1-1	Gulf South Conf. Champs
1977 – Troy State University (Secondary)	6-4	
1978 – Troy State University (Secondary)	8-2	
1979 – Air Force Academy (Secondary)	2-9	
1980 – Air Force Academy (Secondary)	7-4	
1981 – Air Force Academy (Defensive Coordinator)	4-7	
1982 – Air Force Academy (Defensive Coordinator)	8-5	Won Hall of Fame Bowl
1983 – Troy State University (Head Coach)	7-4	
1984 – Troy State University (Head Coach)	12-1	NCAA Division II Champion
1985 – Denver Broncos (Special Teams/Defensive Assistant)	11-5	(2nd AFC West)
1986 – Denver Broncos (Special Teams/Tight Ends)	11-5 (1st AFC West)	AFC Champ (Lost SBXXI)
1987 – Denver Broncos (Tight Ends/Wide Receivers)	10-4-1 (1st AFC West)	AFC Champ (Lost SBXXII)
1988 – Denver Broncos (Quarterbacks)	8-8 (2nd AFC West)	
1989 – Denver Broncos (Offensive Coord./Wide Receivers)	11-5 (1st AFC West)	AFC Champ (Lost SBXXIV)
1990 – Denver Broncos (Offensive Coord./Wide Receivers)	5-11 (5th AFC West)	
1991 – Birmingham Fire (Head Coach)	5-5	Lost First Round Playoff Game
1992 – Birmingham Fire (Head Coach)	7-2-1	Lost First Round Playoff Game
1993 – Samford University (Head Coach)	5-6	
1994 – Pittsburgh Steelers (Wide Receivers)	12-4 (1st AFC Central)	Lost AFC Championship Game
1995 – Pittsburgh Steelers (Wide Receivers)	11-5 (1st AFC Central)	AFC Champ (Lost SBXXX)
1996 – Pittsburgh Steelers (Offensive Coordinator)	10-6 (1st AFC Central)	Lost Second Rd. Playoff Game
1997 – Pittsburgh Steelers (Offensive Coordinator)	11-5 (1st AFC Central)	Lost AFC Championship Game

Record as a coach:	
College assistant record (nine seasons)	60-39-1
College Head Coach record (three seasons)	24-11-0
World League Head Coach record (two seasons)	12-7-1
NFL assistant record – regular season (10 seasons)	100-58-1
NFL assistant record – postseason total	11-7-0
Career Total (24 seasons)	207-122-3

Joe Avezzano
Special Teams

Consistency, big plays and an ability to positively affect the outcome of games have characterized the Cowboys special teams under Joe Avezzano's direction. Avezzano's efforts and excellence have not gone without notice. In eight seasons with the Cowboys, he has twice (1991 and 1993) been named the NFL's Special Teams Coach of the Year.

The Cowboys were one of just three teams in the NFL to be ranked in the Top 13 in the four major kicking game categories in 1997. Dallas led the NFL in kickoff coverage, was fourth in kickoff return average, eleventh in punt return average and thirteenth in punt coverage. Dallas' productivity came on the legs of a new punter and kickoff man in rookie Toby Gowin, as well as a first-year kicker in Richie Cunningham. Cunningham, who earned All-Pro honors, finished the season ranked second in the NFL in scoring.

Before coming to Dallas, Avezzano coached offensive line for four seasons at Texas A&M. He took on the additional duties of offensive coordinator in 1988.

Before joining the Aggies, Avezzano was the head coach at Oregon State (1980-84); offensive coordinator at Tennessee (1977-79); and offensive line coach at Pittsburgh (1973-76).

Avezzano began his coaching career at Washington High School in Massilon, OH, in 1967. He then coached at Florida State for a season before joining Iowa State in 1969.

Avezzano was born in Yonkers, NY (11/17/43) and grew up in Miami. After starring at offensive guard for Florida State, Avezzano was drafted by the Boston Patriots (1966). Joe and wife Diann have a son, Anthony.

Jim Bates
Asst. Head Coach / Defensive Line

In two seasons with the Cowboys, the results of Jim Bates' work with the linebackers have been readily apparent. In 1998, he takes his skills a little closer to the line of scrimmage as the team's defensive line coach, while also adding the responsibilities of assistant head coach to his duties.

His work with the Dallas linebackers in 1996 and 1997 was instrumental in effectively meshing new veterans with inexperienced rookies while improving the club's overall NFL defensive ranking from third in 1996 to second in 1997. The Cowboys also allowed just 20 touchdowns in 1996, the second lowest figure in the NFL.

Prior to joining the Cowboys, Bates, who is entering his 28th year of coaching, had earned NFL coaching experience with stops in Cleveland (1991-93, 1995) and Atlanta (1994). Bates was the defensive coordinator for the San Antonio Gunslingers in 1984, and in 1985, he was promoted to head coach. In 1986, he served as the defensive coordinator for the Arizona Outlaws. In 1988, he was an assistant coach with the Detroit Drive of the Arena League.

Bates also had collegiate coaching jobs at Tennessee (1989), Florida (1990), Texas Tech (1978-83), West Virginia (1977), Kansas State (1975-76), Villanova (1973-74) and Southern Mississippi (1972). Prior to that, he was a graduate assistant at his alma mater, Tennessee (1968), and the head coach at Sevier County, Tenn., High School.

A linebacker for the Vols, Bates graduated from Tennessee in 1969 with a degree in physical education. He is a 1964 graduate of Oxford, Mich., High School.

Dave Campo
Defensive Coordinator

Dave Campo enters his fourth season as the Dallas Cowboys defensive coordinator, and in his three years as coordinator, the Cowboys have finished no lower than ninth in total defense. Last season, the Dallas defense was ranked second overall in the NFL (allowing 282.3 yards-per-game), while leading the entire league in pass defense (157.6).

His 1996 defense closed the year ranked third overall and they surrendered just 20 touchdowns, the second best total in the NFL. His 1995 defense played a prominent role in the team's Super Bowl XXX win over Pittsburgh and finished the season ranked ninth in the NFL in total defense.

Campo, an assistant on the Dallas staff since 1989, spent the four seasons before his promotion as the team's secondary coach, helping that unit grow into one of the team's deepest and most productive units.

Prior to joining the Cowboys in 1989, Campo guided the secondary at the University of Miami, where he coached 1987 Jim Thorpe Award winner Bennie Blades.

His vast experience in the college assistant coaching ranks includes stops at Syracuse (1984-86), Iowa State (1983), Weber State (1981-82), Oregon State (1980), Boise State (1977-79), Washington State (1976), Pitt (1975), Bridgeport (1974) and Albany State (1973).

He began his coaching career at his alma mater, Central Connecticut State (1971-72), where he played football and baseball.

David Cross Campo (6/18/47) is a native of Groton, CT. He and wife Kay have six children – Angie, Eric, Becky, Tommy, Shelbie and Michael.

The next best thing to being on the team

If you're a big fan and always show your team spirit, then stop by Kmart to discover a large variety of NFL team merchandise. From hats to sweatshirts, you'll find quality team apparel at prices that are well under your personal salary cap. So hurry over to your local Kmart. After all, it's football season…suit up and get in the game.

George Edwards
Linebackers

Taking over the assistant coaching duties for linebackers this season is George Edwards, a newcomer to the NFL, but a highly regarded eight-year veteran as a defensive coach in the college ranks. His focus in Dallas will be on the continued growth of youngsters Dexter Coakley and Randall Godfrey at the outside linebacker positions, while continuing the solid play of veteran middle linebacker Fred Strickland.

Edwards spent last season as the defensive line coach at the University of Georgia, where the Bulldogs went 10-2 and finished the season ranked 10th in the final Associated Press rankings.

In 1996, Edwards was the inside linebackers coach at Duke, his alma mater. He joined the Blue Devils after four seasons at Appalachian State University, where he coached outside linebackers for two seasons in 1992-93 before taking over responsibility for all linebackers in 1994-95. While at Appalachian State, he coached Coakley, a two-time Division I-AA National Defensive Player of the Year at ASU and an all-rookie selection as a third round draft choice of the Cowboys in 1997.

Edwards began his coaching career working with linebackers as a graduate assistant at the University of Florida in 1991-92.

A 1989 Duke graduate, Edwards earned four letters as a linebacker with the Blue Devils. He led the team with 116 tackles in his senior season, a year the Blue Devils tied for the Atlantic Coast Conference crown and made an appearance in the All-American Bowl.

A native of Siler City, NC , Edwards was a three-time all-conference and all-county choice at Jordan-Matthews High School.

Buddy Geis
Quarterbacks

Buddy Geis comes to Dallas as the Cowboys new quarterbacks coach after serving as an offensive assistant/assistant quarterback coach for the Indianapolis Colts the last two seasons.

In Geis' two years with the Colts, quarterback Jim Harbaugh recorded the second and fifth best quarterback ratings of his 11-year career.

Prior to joining the Colts, Geis was the offensive coordinator for the Canadian Football League's Memphis Mad Dogs in 1995. He was the offensive coordinator at Tulane (1994) and Duke (1993) after breaking into the NFL as the Green Bay Packers receivers coach under Lindy Infante from 1988-91.

Geis' star pupil with the Packers, Sterling Sharpe, reached 200 career receptions faster than any other receiver in Packers' history. Sharpe also became the first Packer since Don Hutson in 1945 to lead the NFL in receptions when he tallied 90 catches in his second year in the league (1989). Sharpe earned a spot on the NFC Pro Bowl squad in both 1989 and 1990.

Geis was the Memphis State Tigers' offensive coordinator and quarterbacks coach (1986-87) prior to his stint with the Packers. He got his first pro coaching experience with the USFL's Jacksonville Bulls from 1984-85. He first worked with Infante while coaching at Tulane (1977-82) after a stop at Arizona (1974-76). Geis started his coaching career at Altoona, PA, High School from 1971-73.

He saw action as a freshman wide receiver at Northern Arizona before transferring to Lock Haven University and earning a degree in health and physical education.

Buddy and wife Jere have two children, Adam and Jeni.

Steve Hoffman
Kickers/Quality Control

Steve Hoffman solidified his reputation around the NFL for his ability to identify and develop young kickers and punters in 1997. With Richie Cunningham earning All-Pro honors in his first-year in the NFL and Toby Gowin among the top rookie punters, Hoffman continued his successful string of providing Dallas an outstanding kicking game in 1997.

Since joining the Cowboys in 1989, Hoffman has recruited three rookie free agent placekickers to the Cowboys. All three of those players—Ken Willis, Lin Elliott and Chris Boniol—made the Dallas roster and kicked at least 18 field goals in their first NFL season. Punter John Jett also came to the Cowboys via the rookie free agent route, and Hoffman helped develop him into a four-year veteran who performed consistently for two Super Bowl Championship clubs in Dallas.

After joining the Cowboys to coach kickers in 1989, Hoffman added the duties of quality control in 1990.

From 1985-87 Hoffman oversaw kickers at the University of Miami and was a top instructor for Ray Pelfrey's kicking camps.

For two springs Hoffman coached in Italy as offensive coordinator of the Bellusco Blackhawks in 1987 and the Rho Blacknights in 1988. In the fall of 1988, he coached at Sunset High School in Miami.

After punting with the Washington Federals of the USFL in 1983, Hoffman went to training camp with the Redskins in 1981 and 1983, Seattle in 1984 and New Orleans in 1985.

Born in Camden, NJ (9/8/58), Hoffman starred in baseball and football at York Suburban High School in York, PA. He earned All-Mid-Atlantic Conference honors at Dickinson College.

Hudson Houck
Offensive Line

In five seasons with Dallas, Hudson Houck has molded the Cowboys offensive line into one of the top units in club history. During his Dallas tenure, the Cowboys offensive line has surrendered just 125 sacks and is one of just four teams in the NFL to have allowed fewer than 40 sacks in each of the last five seasons. The 125 sacks allowed from 1993-97 were the fewest in the NFL - New England is second with 132 sacks allowed over that same span.

The Dallas line has led the NFC in fewest sacks allowed in three of Houck's five seasons, and in all, six of his linemen have made 16 trips to the Pro Bowl in the last five years. During his 15-year NFL career, his lines have also helped running backs produce six NFL rushing titles and 13 1,000-yard rushing seasons.

Houck spent the 1992 season as the offensive line coach for the Seattle Seahawks. Prior to that, he was the offensive line coach for the Los Angeles Rams (1983 to 1991). While with the Rams, five of his linemen made a combined 21 trips to the Pro Bowl.

Before entering the NFL, Houck served as an assistant coach in the college ranks at Southern California (1970-71), Stanford (1972-75) and a second tour of duty with USC (1976-82) under head coach John Robinson.

Prior to graduating, Houck played three seasons as a center at USC. He was a reserve on the Trojans' 1962 National Championship team.

Houck (1/7/43) is a native of Los Angeles, where he attended Eagle Rock High School.

Jim Jeffcoat
Defensive Line Assistant

Former Cowboys defensive end Jim Jeffcoat returns to Dallas to work with Jim Bates as the Cowboys assistant defensive line coach. Jeffcoat will be bringing 15 years of NFL playing experience to the coaching staff this fall.

Jeffcoat joins the coaching ranks this season after finishing his playing career in Buffalo following the 1997 season. He retired from the league with 102.5 career sacks and 745 tackles. He played in 227 career games, which places him among the top 40 NFL players all-time in terms of number of games played.

Jeffcoat spent the first 12 years of his career with Dallas after being selected in the first round of the 1983 NFL Draft, and he was a member of the Cowboys' teams that won Super Bowls XXVII and XXVIII. By joining Chan Gailey's staff, Jeffcoat has played for or coached with all four head coaches in Cowboys history.

During his stint with the Cowboys, Jeffcoat totaled 698 tackles and 94.5 sacks. His best season in Dallas was 1989, when he finished with a career-high 100 tackles, 11.5 sacks and a career-high three fumble recoveries. Jeffcoat tied the Cowboys team record for sacks in a game when he registered five sacks at Washington on Nov. 10, 1985.

Jeffcoat was a three-year starter at Arizona State University from 1980-82, where he earned All-Pac 10 and honorable mention All-America honors. Jeffcoat earned All-America football honors at Matawan, NJ, Regional High School.

He and wife Tammy have a son, Jaren, and twins, Jackson and Jacqueline.

Joe Juraszek
Strength and Conditioning

Joe Juraszek joined Dallas in February, 1997 as the Cowboys strength and conditioning coach. Now is his second year, it is obvious that the players respect his program and are excited to follow it. Juraszek's hands-on approach stresses strength development, cardiovascular work, flexibility and speed work. He works with the players to tailor programs to individual player needs based on the player's input and their workout history. Juraszek, along with overseeing the strength and conditioning programs for the team, also works with the Cowboys medical staff implementing rehabilitation programs for injured players.

Juraszek came to Dallas after serving as the University of Oklahoma strength coach from 1993-96. He worked with three different coaching staffs during his four-year tenure at OU, and was faced with the daunting task of taking 1,000 cumulative pounds off the 1994 football team. Juraszek joined the Sooners after serving as the strength coach at Texas Tech University from 1987-92. He was a graduate assistant and then a full-time assistant strength coach for the Sooners from 1981-86.

He attended the University of New Mexico from 1976-81, where he played linebacker and defensive end for the Lobos football team while earning bachelor's degrees in Physical Education/Health and Economics. He added a master's degree in Economics while serving as a graduate assistant strength coach at Oklahoma.

A native of Chicago, IL (6/8/58), Juraszek (pronounced jer-ASS-ick) and his wife Camille have a daughter, Nikki Jo, and a son, J.D.

HOW TO TACKLE AN OSTRICH.

THE SAME WAY YOU **TACKLE** AN **ALLIGATOR**, A **SHARK**, A **SNAKE**, OR A WHOMPIN' BIG OL' LIZARD: WITH A LOT OF EXTREMELY **GOOD HANDS**.

DAN POST ®
A lot of style. A lot of sole.

DAN POST® EXOTIC WESTERN BOOTS WITH THE EXCLUSIVE 7-LAYER CUSHION CRADLE INSOLE. THE BEST LINE IN THE BUSINESS

ACM074/98-6/98

YOU DON'T HAVE TO BE A GIANT TO WORKOUT AT GOLD'S GYM. COWBOYS AND OILERS TRAIN HERE, TOO.

Les Miles
Tight Ends

Coaching the Cowboys young tight end corps this season will be Les Miles, who joins the Dallas staff after serving as Oklahoma State University's offensive coordinator for the past three years.

As Oklahoma State's offensive coordinator (1995-97), Miles improved the Cowboys offense from an average of 310.5 yards and 20.7 points-per-game in 1995 to 375.7 yards and 30.2 points in 1997 while making an appearance in the Alamo Bowl.

Prior to joining the OSU staff, Miles was the offensive line coach for the Michigan Wolverines from 1987-94. During his eight-year stint with the Wolverines, he coached eight first-team All-Americas and 12 NFL draftees, including Steve Everitt, a first-round selection of the Cleveland Browns in 1993, and Joe Cocozzo, a third-round selection of the San Diego Chargers in 1993. The Wolverines played in five Rose Bowls and won an unprecedented five consecutive Big 10 titles during Miles' tenure.

Miles was the offensive line coach for the Colorado Buffaloes from 1983-86 after serving as a Buffaloes' graduate assistant coach in 1982.

Miles was a guard on the Wolverines offensive line from 1972-75, helping Michigan to three Big 10 co-championships and an Orange Bowl berth following the 1975 season. He earned a degree in economics from Michigan. Miles earned all-state honors in football at Elyria, OH, High School while also lettering in baseball and wrestling.

A native of Elyria, OH and a member of the Elyria Hall of Fame, Les (11/10/53) and wife Kathy have a daughter, Kathryn Ann, and a son, Leslie Matthew.

Dwain Painter
Wide Receivers

Dwain Painter enters his 11th season as a NFL assistant coach, and his 31st year in coaching, with the assignment of directing the Dallas Cowboys wide receivers. Painter comes to Dallas after serving one season with the Super Bowl XXXII Champion Denver Broncos.

In Denver, he coordinated the Broncos quality control effort for the defensive unit, while assisting with Denver special teams units.

Prior to joining the Broncos, Painter served as the Chargers' quarterbacks coach from 1994 to 1996. During which time the Chargers captured the AFC title and a trip to the Super Bowl XXIX.

During the 1992 and 1993 seasons, Painter was the wide receivers coach for the Indianapolis Colts.

Painter began his NFL coaching career in 1988 when he became the wide receivers coach of the Pittsburgh Steelers under Chuck Noll. He coached the Steelers wide receivers for four seasons (1988-1991). Prior to his time in Pittsburgh, Painter coached for 17 years on the collegiate level.

Painter broke into the coaching profession as a head coach at Wall, NJ, High School in 1965. He served as an assistant in the collegiate ranks at San Jose State (1971-72), College of San Mateo (1973), Brigham Young (1974-75) and UCLA (1976-78) before becoming the head coach at Northern Arizona (1979-81). Painter then moved on to Georgia Tech (1981-85), Texas (1986) and Illinois (1987) as an assistant.

Painter was a quarterback and defensive back at Rutgers from 1960 to 1963 and was a member of the first undefeated football team (9-0 in 1961) in school history.

Dwain was born on February 13, 1942, in Monroeville, Pennsylvania.

Clancy Pendergast
Defensive Assistant/Quality Control

Clancy Pendergast, who joined the Cowboys in 1996, serves the dual role of defensive assistant/quality control. Pendergast oversees Dallas' defensive quality control and assists linebackers coach George Edwards.

The Cowboys linebackers finished 1997 as the second, third and fourth leading tacklers on the team. Randall Godfrey led the group with 149 tackles while third-round draft choice Dexter Coakley started all year at the weakside linebacker spot and recorded 136 tackles, the club-record for tackles by a rookie. Fred Strickland followed his 153 tackles in 1996 with a 132 tackle performance in 1997.

In 1996, the Dallas linebackers helped improve the Cowboys rush defense from 16th to ninth in the NFL. The linebackers were led by Strickland, who recorded a team-high 153 tackles. Pendergast worked closely with rookie draft pick Godfrey, helping him earn a starting spot at strongside linebacker by Game 11 against Green Bay (11/18/96).

Pendergast spent the 1995 season with the Houston Oilers as a defensive assistant and quality control coach. He joined Houston from Alabama-Birmingham, where he was named the tight ends coach in January of 1995. Prior to his short stint at UAB, Pendergast spent the 1993-94 seasons working with the tight ends and as an advance scout at Oklahoma. In 1992, Pendergast was a defensive assistant at Southern Cal. After earning his bachelor's degree from Arizona (1990), Pendergast worked the 1991 season as a graduate assistant at Mississippi State, helping with the receivers and working as an advance scout.

Pendergast (11/29/67) is a native of Phoenix, AZ.

Tommie Robinson
Offensive Assistant

Although a newcomer to the Cowboys staff in 1998, Tommie Robinson is not a new face around the team, having spent the 1997 training camp with Dallas as one of the recipients of the Jerry Jones Minority Coaching Fellowship. Robinson has also been to camp with the New Orleans Saints and St. Louis Rams.

Robinson joined the Cowboys after just one month on the staff at UNLV. He joined the Rebels after four seasons as wide receivers coach at Texas Christian University (1994-97), where he was part of the Horned Frogs 1994 Southwest Conference Co-Championship team.

Robinson joined TCU after two seasons as running backs coach at Utah State (1992-93), where he helped the Aggies capture the Big West Conference Championship and a Las Vegas Bowl win in 1993.

Prior to Utah State, Robinson spent two years (1989-90) at his alma mater, Troy State, as the linebackers coach, and then one campaign at the University of Arkansas in 1991.

After college, Robinson pursued professional football for a year before breaking into the coaching ranks at the high school level from 1986-88.

Robinson was a three year starter in the secondary at Troy State University (1982-84), and he earned All-Gulf South Conference honors as a senior on the 1984 Division II national championship team under head coach Chan Gailey.

A native of Phenix City, Ala. (4/4/63), Robinson was a four-sport athlete at Central High School. He earned his degree in psychology from Troy State in 1985. He and his wife, Lartonyar, have three children – sons, Dantrell and Trey, and daughter, Towanda.

Clarence Shelmon
Running Backs

Tutoring top-flight running backs is nothing new to Clarence Shelmon, who joins the Cowboys in 1998 after six seasons working with the Seattle Seahawks' running backs. In Dallas, Shelmon will guide one of the NFL's top backfield duos in Emmitt Smith and Daryl Johnston, as well as his former star pupil from Seattle, Chris Warren.

The Cowboys hope Shelmon brings the same level of success to Dallas that he enjoyed in Seattle, where over the last five seasons, Seattle has finished in the top five in the NFL in rushing yards four times.

Shelmon inherited Warren, and helped turn him into a four-time 1,000 yard rusher (1992-95). Shelmon entered the NFL in 1991 as the running backs coach with the Los Angeles Rams before moving on to Seattle in 1992.

Shelmon made the jump to the NFL from the University of Southern California, where he spent four years (1987-90) as the running backs coach. Before joining the Trojans, Shelmon handled the running backs at Arizona from 1984-86.

In all, eight of his backs earned All-Pac 10 honors, including two conference rushing champions and one second place finisher, during his seven years in the Pac-10.

He began his coaching career in 1975 as a graduate assistant at Houston (1975-76). Following a year of coaching at Carroll High School in Corpus Christi, Tex., Shelmon spent three seasons at Army (1978-80) and three at Indiana University (1981-83).

Born in Bossier City, La., on Sept. 17, 1952, he attended Airline High School before moving to the University of Houston, where he was a two-year letterman as a running back.

Mike Zimmer
Defensive Assistant

For the third time in his four years with the Cowboys, Mike Zimmer's secondary helped the Dallas defense finish 1997 as one of the top two pass defenses in the NFL. The Cowboys surrendered only 172.0 passing yards-per-game in 1994 to lead the league in pass defense, while the 1996 defense allowed 175.4 passing yards-per-game to finish second in the league. In 1997, the team returned to the top by allowing a league-low 157.6 yards-per-game.

In 1997, Zimmer was once again able to play one of the top cornerback tandems in the league, Deion Sanders and Kevin Smith, and a Pro Bowl safety, Darren Woodson. This continuity helped the Cowboys defense hold 13 opponents to under 200 yards passing.

Prior to arriving in Dallas, Zimmer spent five seasons (1989-93) as the defensive coordinator/secondary coach at Washington State University. In 1992, the Cougars posted a 9-3 record, including a win in the Copper Bowl, which equaled the second most wins in school history.

Prior to joining the Cougars' staff in 1989, Zimmer was an assistant at Weber State College (1981-88). He began his coaching career as a part-time assistant at the University of Missouri in 1979.

Zimmer was a two-time all-conference quarterback at Lockport, IL, High School in 1972-73. He went on to play quarterback at Illinois State University in 1974. After redshirting the 1975 season, he suffered a broken thumb in the spring of 1976 and was moved to linebacker. A neck injury, suffered during the 1976 season, led to surgery and the end of his playing career.

Ring

Ring

Ring

Ring

Ring

———

Good luck on getting that sixth ring, Dallas.
AT&T. Official telecommunications sponsor of Texas Stadium.

It's all within your reach.

Quarterback

Troy Aikman is entering his 10th NFL season at the Cowboys helm after guiding Dallas to five consecutive NFC Eastern Division titles, four NFC Championship Games and three Super Bowl titles. In 1997, Aikman threw for over 3,000 yards for the third consecutive season and the fifth time in his career. He currently holds or is tied for 42 Dallas passing records, and with each pass he adds to his marks for attempts (3,696), completions (2,292) and passing yards (26,016). In 1998, Aikman will be closing in on the career record for touchdown passes, entering the season with 129.

Danny White holds the club mark at 155, followed by Roger Staubach (153) and Don Meredith (135).

Aikman is the lead player on a quarterback depth chart, but behind him is capable backup Jason Garrett, who enters his sixth season with the Cowboys. Battling for the third spot will be Max Knake, who played collegiately at TCU, and Daniel Gonzalez (East Carolina).

Running Back

Emmitt Smith will again be leading the Cowboys running game in 1998. Smith spent the offseason conditioning and learning the Cowboys new offense from new running backs coach Clarence Shelmon. In 1997, Smith became the fourth player in NFL history to rush for over 1,000 yards in seven consecutive seasons when he gained 1,074 yards and averaged 4.1 yards-per-carry. Smith, currently 11th in NFL career rushing yards, could crack into the top five in 1998, and he has a chance to top Marcus Allen's career rushing touchdowns record of 123.

Chris Warren joins the Cowboys in 1998 to back-up Smith and provide the club a solid veteran back. In eight years with the Seattle Seahawks, Warren posted four 1,000-yard rushing seasons, made three Pro Bowl appearances and left Seattle as the club's all-time rushing leader with 6,706 career yards on the ground.

Fullback Daryl Johnston, noted as the game's premier blocking fullback, is

returning for his 10th year with the team after neck surgery last season. In his nine professional seasons, he had not missed a game until midway through last season. Following his October surgery, Johnston should be healthy and back on the field for the Cowboys in 1998. With Johnston out of the lineup in 1997, fourth-round draft choice Nicky Sualua received valuable experience as a rookie. In 1998, Sualua will be counted on as Johnston's primary back up. Sualua was considered the best pure blocking fullback in the 1997 NFL Draft.

Wide Receiver

For the seventh straight season, Michael Irvin led the team in receiving with 75 receptions for 1,180 yards. It was his sixth career 1,000 yard receiving season. With another great performance in 1998, Irvin has the possibility of climbing as high as seventh on the NFL's all-time list for career receptions and career receiving yards (1,216). Irvin is just one

member of a receiving corps that should open up the Cowboys passing game in 1998. Fourth-year pro Billy Davis will get a chance to show the play-making capabilities he displayed in the 1997 preseason when he led the NFL in receptions and receiving yards.

In addition, the Cowboys signed veteran Ernie Mills and speedster Jimmy Oliver during the off-season, and both players have the ability to make big plays and stretch defenses up the field. Mills registered 39 receptions for 679 yards and eight touchdowns with the Pittsburgh Steelers in their Super Bowl season. After fully recovering from knee surgery following that Super Bowl, Mills should be ready to go this fall.

The Cowboys fourth-round draft choice in 1997, Macey Brooks will be back on the field this summer as well after recovering from a fractured forearm last season. He is a big, speed receiver that coaches expect to battle for playing time in 1998. Third-year man Stepfret Williams showed the club just how valuable a weapon he can be on third downs last season, hauling in 19 third-down passes and converting 15 of them into first downs.

Tight End

The Cowboys enter 1998 with one of their most solid groups of tight ends in years. Eric Bjornson, who assumed the starting tight end position in 1996, will be healthy after spending the offseason rehabilitating his fractured left fibula, in December of 1997. Bjornson finished the year with 47 receptions for 442 yards, and he has collected 95 receptions over the last two seasons.

The Cowboys first-round selection in the 1997 draft was used to select LSU tight end David LaFleur. LaFleur proved himself to be a punishing blocker in just his first NFL season. He also displayed his abilities as a pass catcher with Bjornson injured in December, catching 10 passes for 66 yards and two touchdowns over the final three games.

Seventh-round draft choice Rod Monroe (Cincinnati) will be given every opportunity to continue learning the intricacies of the game after making the transition from basketball to football his senior season.

Offensive Line

With the return of three Pro Bowl linemen (Erik Williams, Larry Allen and Nate Newton) and a year under Clay Shiver's belt as the starting center, the Cowboys offensive line looks to be as strong as ever in 1998. The only change in the make-up of the line will be at right guard, where free agent Everett McIver joins the club after two seasons with the Miami Dolphins.

Dallas used a second-round draft choice to select tackle Flozell Adams (Michigan State). Oliver Ross (Iowa State) and Antonio Fleming (Georgia) will give the team a strong nucleus of young talent. Adams will be battling second-year tackle Tony Hutson for the top reserve position.

In 1997, the Cowboys offensive line surrendered only 39 sacks on 592 passing plays, or one every 15 plays. In addition, Emmitt Smith was able to rush for over 1,000 for the seventh consecutive season, making it possible for Larry Allen (third) and Erik Williams (third) to be selected to the Pro Bowl.

Defensive Line

The Cowboys will enter the 1998 season with some new faces joining some seasoned veterans on the defensive line. Leon Lett and Chad Hennings will open the season as the club's starting defensive tackles. This duo should make things interesting for teams in the middle. Hennings will be manning the left tackle spot after recording 4.5 sacks and 52 tackles in 1997. Lett, who only saw action in the club's final three games in 1997,

Your Personal Financial Worksheet

We have the right financing tools to cut your monthly payments in half! Use this worksheet to total your current monthly payment, then give us a call.

Dan Marino, *All-Pro Quarterback*
Spokesperson for FIRSTPLUS Financial

	Outstanding Balance	Monthly Payment
Mortgage Loan	$	$
Car Loan	$	$
Department Store	$	$
Department Store	$	$
Credit Card	$	$
College Tuition	$	$
Personal Loans	$	$
Other Credit	$	$
Your Total Current Monthly Payment	$	

SPECIAL NUMBER FOR NFL FANS **1-888-561-MORE**

will be looking to return to the form that landed him in the Pro Bowl following the 1994 season. Dallas addressed the future of its defensive line by drafting defensive tackle Michael Myers (Alabama) in the fourth round. He will join last year's fourth rounder Antonio Anderson, who exploded onto the scene in 1997 with 40 tackles and two sacks to earn All-Rookie honors. Hurvin McCormack and Darren Benson will be competing for roster spots as reserve tackles in 1998.

At defensive end, the new faces surface. Third year pro Kavika Pittman, and 1998 first-round draft choice Greg Ellis will team up on the outsides to give Dallas a young and exciting pair of ends. Pittman, the Cowboys top choice in 1996, has displayed flashes of potential in his limited playing time, and in 1998 he will get every chance to expand on that playing time with the starting job. Joining Pittman at end will be Ellis, who left the University of North Carolina with a school-record 32.5 career sacks — this from the same school that produced Lawrence Taylor. Broderick Thomas, who can move between linebacker and defensive end, will be available to provide a veteran presence to the team's pressure front, and the versatile McCormack will also see playing time at end.

Linebackers

The Cowboys linebacking group enters 1998 as solid as ever. Dallas returns all three members of its 1997 starting linebacker corps. Middle linebacker Fred Strickland will again be calling the defensive signals after posting 132 tackles in 1997. He finished last season with seven double-digit tackle games after suffering through a mid-season injury. Randall Godfrey will begin his third NFL campaign as the Cowboys starting strongside linebacker, a position from which he logged 149 tackles to lead this group. The final piece to the linebacking puzzle is All-Rookie selection Dexter Coakley, who jumped into the fray in his first season and established a club record for tackles by a rookie with 136.

New to the club in 1998 will be fifth-

round draft choice Darren Hambrick (South Carolina), who will bring some much-needed depth to the linebacking position.

Defensive Backs

The Cowboys secondary is the strongest returning position group on the defensive side of the ball. The secondary is anchored by, arguably, the best pair of cornerbacks in the league. Deion Sanders, who was selected to his sixth Pro Bowl in 1997, and Kevin Smith led the 1996 defense to a No. 1 pass defense ranking, surrendering only 157.6 passing yards-per-game.

Second-year cornerback Kevin Mathis and Wendell Davis will be expected to provide quality depth.

Strong safety Darren Woodson enters the 1998 season on the heels of his fourth career Pro Bowl selection. With the free agency departure of free safety Brock Marion in the offseason, that spot is up for grabs this fall. A number of worthy candidates are lined up to fight for the right to start. Veteran George Teague returns to the club in 1998 after a year away in Miami. Teague started 10 games at free safety for Dallas in 1996 when Marion was lost to a shoulder injury. Also vying for the position is second-year pro Omar Stoutmire, who, along with his work in the nickel package, started two games for Woodson at strong safety in 1997 and finished the season with 76 tackles.

Also in the picture is Kenny Wheaton, a 1997 draft choice at cornerback, Charlie Williams, who is a key member of the club's third down schemes, and Singor Mobley, who had a strong rookie year on special teams.

Dallas added depth to the safety position by drafting Izell Reese (Alabama-Birmingham), who will see most of his action on special teams.

Special Teams

The Cowboys enter 1998 after having completely retooled their special teams in 1997. After losing kicker Chris Boniol (Philadelphia) and punter John Jett (Detroit) to free agency, Richie

Cunningham and Toby Gowin won jobs as their replacements and had outstanding campaigns. Cunningham earned Associated Press All-Pro honors and Gowin established three separate club records for punting.

The Cowboys were one of just three teams in the NFL to be ranked in the top 13 in all four major special teams categories. With the help of safety Charlie Williams and wide receiver Billy Davis, Dallas led the NFL in kickoff coverage. Williams tied for seventh in the NFL in 1997 with 26 special teams tackles, while Davis finished the year with 20.

troy aikman

6-4 ★ 219 ★ BORN: 11/21/66
HENRYETTA, OK ★ UCLA ★
10TH SEASON ★ D-1 FOR 1989

QUARTERBACK

Troy Aikman's success has mirrored that of the Cowboys during his nine years as the team's quarterback...he guided the team to five straight NFC East titles (1992-96), four NFC title games (1992-95) and three Super Bowl titles...in the process he now holds or is tied for 42 Dallas passing records, including career marks for attempts (3,696), completions (2,292), passing yards (26,016) and completion percentage (62.0)...finished third in the NFC, eighth in the NFL, in passing yards with 3,283 in 1997, marking the fifth time in his career he has passed for over 3,000 yards in a season...holds the NFL career postseason record for completion percentage (66.5%)...has posted an 11-2 mark as a starter in the postseason...is 10th on the NFL's all-time quarterback list with a career quarterback rating of 82.32...has posted an 87-55 record (.613) in 142 career starts...earned his sixth straight trip to the Pro Bowl following the 1996 season.

Passing	Att.	Comp.	Yards	Pct.	TD	Int	Long	Sks/Yds	Rating
1997	518	292	3,283	56.4	19	12	64t	33/269	78.0
Career	3,696	2,292	26,016	62.0	129	110	90	218/1,469	82.3

COWBOYS

34

larry Allen

6-3 ★ 326 ★ BORN: 11/27/71
NAPA, CA ★ SONOMA STATE
5th SEASON ★ D-2 FOR 1994

GUARD

In three seasons as a full-time starter at right guard, Larry Allen has become one of the NFL's finest young offensive linemen...started every game for the third consecutive season...earned his third spot in the Pro Bowl and was a consensus All-Pro selection...joins Randall McDaniel (Minnesota) and Bruce Matthews (Tennessee) as the only guards to have been selected to each of the last three Pro Bowl teams...one of seven members of the NFC and AFC offensive lines on this year's Pro Bowl squad to be making his third straight appearance... has shown versatility by moving between right tackle (1994), right guard (1995-97) and left tackle (1997)...part of a group that has allowed just 96 sacks in 64 games, fewest in the NFL during that time (Kansas City is second with 99 sacks allowed)... has also been a member of an offensive unit that has posted the three lowest sacks allowed totals in club history with 18 in 1995, 19 in 1996 and 20 in 1994.

1997 GAMES/STARTS:	16/16
CAREER GAMES/STARTS:	64/58

COWBOYS

antonio anderson

6-6 ★ 318
BORN: 6/4/73 ★ MILFORD, CT
SYRACUSE ★ 2ND SEASON
D4a FOR 1997

DEFENSIVE TACKLE

A steal with the fifth pick (101st overall) in the fourth round of the 1997 NFL Draft...a defensive tackle that provided depth along the defensive line and contributed in his first year...earned a spot in the defensive tackle rotation and earned All Rookie honors...his two sacks in 1997 were the most by a Dallas rookie since Russell Maryland in 1991...his five starts marked the first time a rookie had started along the Dallas defensive line since Maryland started the final seven games of 1991...had a solid rookie season — 40 tackles, two sacks and two passes defensed...on the first snap of his NFL career, recorded half a sack of Steelers QB Kordell Stewart...recorded a season-high seven tackles against Philadelphia (9/15)...earned first NFL start against Chicago (9/28)...has three cousins who have played pro sports - Stanford Jennings (former Cincinnati Bengals running back), Keith Jennings (former Chicago Bears tight end) and John Salley (former Miami Heat forward - NBA).

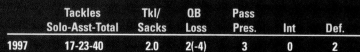

	Tackles Solo-Asst-Total	Tkl/ Sacks	Q.B Loss	Pass Pres.	Int	Def.
1997	17-23-40	2.0	2(-4)	3	0	2

COWBOYS

GERMAN CAR
HEADQUARTERS

1997 Porsche Turbo S, Blk/Blk, 4K miles

1996 Porsche Twin Turbo, Speed Yellow/Cash, 4K mi, Loaded! Several Others in Stock!!

1998 Porsche 993 Cabriolet, Silver/Boxster Red, Last of the Air Cooled Engines!

1996 Porsche 993 Coupe, Black Metallic/Grey, 14K miles. Great Selection of 90-98 911's!

1998 Porsche Boxster in stock or Custom Order or Call!

1999 Porsche 996 Cabriolet & Coupe Buy from Stock or Custom Order Yours Today!

1998 Mercedes SL600, 2K miles Others in Stock '90-'98!

PORSCHE

99 911 Carrera Coupe, Black/Black	NEW
99 911 Carrera Coupe, Arena Red/Beige	NEW
99 911 Carrera Coupe, Ocean Blue/Black	NEW
99 911 Carrera Coupe, Black/Beige	NEW
99 911 Carrera Coupe, Black Met./Black	NEW
99 911 Carrera Coupe, Guards Red/Beige	NEW
99 911 Carrera Coupe, Silver/Black	NEW
99 911 Carrera Coupe, Guards Red/Beige	200 mi.
99 Boxster	TAKING ORDERS
98 911 Carrera Cab, Silver/Grey	800 mi.
98 911 Carrera 2S, Red/Black	5K mi.
97 911 Carrera Targa, Zenith Blue/Grey	2K mi.
97 911 Turbo, Silver/Cashmere	2K mi.
97 911 Carrera 2S, Silver/Black	7K mi.
96 911 Turbo, Speed Yellow/Cash	4K mi.
96 911 Carrera Coupe, Polar Silver/Blue	8K mi.
95 928 GTS, Auto, Black/Cashmere	23K mi.
95 911 Carrera Cab, Black/Grey, 18"	12K mi.
95 911 Carrera Cab, Black/Black	2K mi.
94 Turbo 3.6, Red/Cashmere	10K mi.
94 968 Coupe, Tip, Black/Black	33K mi.
93 928 GTS, 5-spd, Black/Cashmere	28K mi.
87 944, Red/Black	44K mi.

MERCEDES-BENZ

98 SL500 Sport, Red/Parch, Xenon, CD, HS	2K mi.
98 CLK 320, Black/Black	2K mi.
98 SLK 230, Yellow/Black, Phone, CD	2K mi.
98 ML 320, Black/Grey	3K mi.
97 E60, Black/Black, New	AUG. DEL
97 SL500 Anniv. Ed., Red/Parch, CD, Phone	4K mi.
97 E320, Silver/Grey	12K mi.
97 E420, Smoke Silver/Parchment	8K mi.
97 E420, Silver/Grey	12K mi.
97 E420, Silver/Grey	23K mi.
97 E320, Silver/Grey	13K mi.
97 C36, Black/Black, ASR, CD, Htd Sts	8K mi.
96 S420V, White/Grey, CD	18K mi.
96 E320, Silver/Grey	13K mi.
96 SL500, Imperial Red/Parchment	12K mi.
95 SL500, Imperial Red/Parchment	8K mi.
95 SL500, White/Blue	33K mi.
94 S500 Coupe, Spruce Grn/Parchment	25K mi.
94 S350 Diesel, Black/Grey	81K mi.
94 E500, Silver/Black	50K mi.
94 E320 Cab, Imperial Red/Parchment	15K mi.
93 600SEL, Silver/Grey	28K mi.
90 560SEC, White/Palomino	45K mi.
89 560SEC, 6.0 AMG, Anthracite/Palomino	NICE
89 560 SL, Black Pearl/Grey	43K mi.
85 380SL, Light Ivory/Palomino	52K mi.

1997 BMW 750iL, Black/Black, 12K mi, Navigation System. Big Selection of 7 Series!

Mercedes Benz E60 RS RennTech 6.0 ltr/420HP, 0-60 in 4.9 seconds! Awesome!

1995 BMW 850Csi We have several with low miles...CALL!!

BMW

98 750iL, White/Sand, Navigation	NEW
98 540i Sport, Auto/6-speed	IN STOCK
98 528i Sport	IN STOCK
98 M3A Conv, Black/Black	IN STOCK
98 MZ3, Cosmos Black/Grey, CD	400 mi.
97 740 iL, Oxford Green/Sand	5K mi.
97 740IL, White/Sand, Prem. Snd, HS	17K mi.
97 540i, 6-Spd, Cosmos Blk/Blk, Prem Snd	18K mi.
97 Z3A 2.8, Atlanta Blue/Tan	4K mi.
97 Z3A 2.8, Silver/Black	5K mi.
96 750iL, Black/Sand	15K mi.
96 318ti, Black/Black	20K mi.
95 740iL, Ascot Grn/Sand,ASC, Prem. Snd	14K mi.
93 325ic, Green/Tan	46K mi.
88 M6, Black/Grey	46K mi.
88 M6, Red/Tan	75K mi.

1998 Mercedes SLK Great Selection Available Today

1963 Jaguar XKE, Red/Black, Matching Numbers!!

1998 BMW M3 Convertible 95-98 Models Always in Stock!!!

1967 Shelby GT 500, Center Headlight, 4-speed, Very NICE!!!

Classic MERCEDES-BENZ

77 600 Pullman, 4 dr, Blk/Beige leather	26K mi.
72 600, Astral Silver/Black leather, S/R	9K mi.
72 600, Metallic Blue/Blue leather, S/R	21K mi.
72 600, Grey Beige Met./Brown lthr, S/R	35K mi.
72 600, Black/Cognac leather, S/R	80K mi.
71 280SE 3.5 Conv., Dk. Olive/Cognac	41K mi.
70 600, Anthracite/Black lthr, S/R	75K mi.
69 280SE Conv., White/Cognac	39K mi.
68 600 Pullman Landaulet, Black/Black lthr	3K mi.
66 600 Pullman, 6 dr, M. Blue/Blue lthr, S/R	Restored
62 300SL, Graphite Grey/Red, disc brakes	Restored
61 300d Cabriolet D, Black/Red, 15K mi.	Restored
57 300Sc Cabriolet, Black/Red	Restored
56 300c Cabriolet D, Silver/Black	Restored

OTHERS

98 Audi A8 Quattro 4.2	8K mi.
95 Ferrari F355 Spider, Red/Tan	7K mi.
95 Ferrari F355 B, Black/Tan	4K mi.
96 Jaguar XJ6, Black/Tan	26K mi.
89 Jaguar XJS, Blue Metallic/Tan	52K mi.
89 Lamborghini Countach, Red/Tan, Wing	12K mi.
95 Lexus LS 400, Pearl White/Beige	29K mi.
97 Mitsubishi 3000, Red/Blk, 5-spd, CD	14K mi.
96 Range Rover 4.6 HSE, White/Tan	22K mi.
67 Shelby GT 500, White/Black, Restored	$39K
94 Toyota Landcruiser, Green/Grey Lthr	38K mi.

ISRINGHAUSEN
AUTHORIZED DEALER
BMW

RENNTech

229 East Jefferson. Springfield, IL 62701
Ph:217-528-2277 Fax:217-528-8146
Website: www.isringhausen.com e-mail: gisring@prodigy.net

darren benson

6-7 ★ 308 ★ BORN: 8/25/74
MEMPHIS, TN
TRINITY VALLEY C.C.
4TH SEASON ★ S3 FOR 1995

DEFENSIVE TACKLE

Based on his size and speed, the Cowboys have high hopes for Darren Benson this season as he continues to develop as a defensive tackle...has gained valuable experience and confidence in his three seasons under Chad Hennings and Leon Lett...just 24 years old despite entering his fourth year in the NFL...at 6-7, 308 pounds is the largest player on the defensive side of the ball for Dallas...saw his first game action of 1997 against Chicago (9/28) after having missed the entire 1996 season with an ACL tear in his left knee...had a tackle and a tackle for a loss the next week at Washington (10/13)...closed out the season on a high note when he tied for the team lead among defensive linemen with four tackles at Cincinnati (12/14)...selected in the third-round of the 1995 NFL Supplemental Draft out of Trinity Valley Community College...pairs with Lett to create one of the most formidable field goal rush pairs in the NFL.

	Tackles Solo-Asst.-Total	Tkl/ Loss	QB Pres.	Pass Def.
1997	5-2-7	1(-2)	0	0
Career	7-4-11	1(-2)	0	0

COWBOYS

eric bjornson

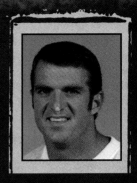

6-4 ★ 236
BORN: 12/15/71 ★ OAKLAND, CA
WASHINGTON ★ 4th SEASON
D-4a FOR 1995

TIGHT END

When called on in 1996, Eric Bjornson immediately stepped on the field and displayed his soft hands and ability to run concise pass routes…similar in size (6-4, 236-pounds) and speed (4.5 40-yard dash) to Jay Novacek…in the last two seasons, the Cowboys have discovered they have quite a weapon in this pass catching tight end…as a rookie learned the position from one of the best in Novacek…had played the position for just one year, before posting impressive numbers in 1996-97…has 102 receptions for 883 yards and three touchdowns over three seasons…prior to fracturing his left fibula against Carolina in December was second in the NFC and sixth in the NFL among tight ends with 47 receptions…was also second in the NFC, ninth in the NFL, in receiving yards by a tight end with 442…despite the injury, finished 1997 second on the team with 47 receptions and was third with 442 yards.

Receiving	No.	Yards	Avg.	Long	TD
1997	47	442	9.4	32	0
Career	102	883	8.7	32	3

COWBOYS

NFL Photo of the Year
Super Bowl Sunday 1998
Photography by Rich Clarkson and Associates

macey brooks

6-5 ★ 220 ★ BORN: 2/2/75
HAMPTON, VA
JAMES MADISON ★ 2ND SEASON
D-4b FOR 1997

WIDE RECEIVER

A receiver with the size and strength to win battles against cornerbacks and safeties when the football is up for grabs...at 6-5, 220-pounds, not only has the size to protect the ball from opposing defenders, but also the ability to be an effective blocker for Emmitt Smith in the running game...expected to battle for serious playing time in his second season...one of nine rookie draft choices to make the roster in 1997...recorded seven receptions for 98 yards and a touchdown in the first three preseason contests before suffering a fractured right forearm against St. Louis (8/15)...placed on injured reserved following surgery and sat out entire season...had 118 receptions for 2,014 yards and 25 touchdowns during his college career...led the team with 828 receiving yards as a senior...was twice selected in the Major League Baseball Draft (San Francisco Giants–second round, 1993 as a high school senior and Kansas City Royals–55th round, 1996)

COWBOYS

dexter coakley

5-10 ★ 215 ★ BORN: 10/20/72
MT. PLEASANT, SC
APPALACHIAN STATE
2ND SEASON ★ D-3a FOR 1997

LINEBACKER

Entered the NFL as a third round draft choice and was expected to win a starting job at the weakside linebacker position...did so with relative ease...provided a spark for the NFL's second ranked defensive unit all year...what he lacks in size, he more than makes up for in quickness, speed (4.47) and intensity...was the first of five rookies to start for Dallas in 1997...was the NFL's leader among all rookies in tackles with 136 stops—a total that was third on the Cowboys defensive list—and set a Dallas record for tackles by a rookie...named to the All Rookie teams that were selected by *Pro Football Weekly* and *Football News*...was the club leader in tackles for a loss with 10 stops for losses totaling 11 yards...was the NFL's Rookie of the Month for October...reached double figures in tackles in six of the final eight games and seven times for the season.

	Tackles Solo-Asst.—Total	Sacks	Tkl/ Loss	QB Pres.	Pass Int	Def.	Fumbles For.-Rec.	Special Teams Solo-Asst. — Total
1997	68-68—136	2.5	10(-11)	4	1	3	1-1	6-1—7

COWBOYS

43

richie cunningham

5-10 ★ 167
BORN: 8/18/70 ★ HOUMA, LA
SOUTHWESTERN LOUISIANA,
2ND SEASON ★ FA FOR 1997

KICKER

The Cowboys lost one of the most accurate kickers in NFL history to free agency following the 1996 season when Chris Boniol left for Philadelphia, so they once again dipped into the free agent pool to find Richie Cunningham...proved to be as accurate as his predecessor...finished the 1997 season second in the NFL in field goal accuracy, connecting on 91.9% of his attempts (34-of-37)...was the second highest field goal percentage in team history...registered the Cowboys third longest streak of consecutive field goals made by connecting on 18 straight attempts...earned All-Pro honors from Associated Press...34 field goals led the NFL, and 37 field goal attempts tied for the NFC lead, third in the NFL...opened his NFL career by connecting on a career-long 53-yard field goal in the season opener...earned NFC Special Teams Player of the Month honors for September by connecting on 15-of-16 field goal attempts and tying for the NFL lead with 53 points in four games.

SCORING

Year	PAT	FG	Long	Points
1997	24-24	34-37	53	126

FIELD GOAL ACCURACY

Year	11-19	20-29	30-39	40-49	50+	Total	Pct.
1997	1-1	16-16	9-9	7-10	1-1	34-37	.919

COWBOYS

44

billy davis

6-1 ★ 205
BORN: 7/6/72 ★ EL PASO, TX
PITTSBURGH ★ 4TH SEASON
FREE AGENT FOR 1995

WIDE RECEIVER

Came to the Cowboys in 1995 as an unheralded and undrafted talent out of Pittsburgh, a long-shot to make the team at wide receiver...went on to earn a roster spot in training camp with his football instincts and a valuable ability to play special teams...three years later is still showing coaches he has the ability to help this team in many areas...will be competing for the starting wide receiver spot opposite Michael Irvin this season...led the NFL in preseason with 23 receptions and 403 yards in 1997...also tied for second in the NFL with three touchdowns and led the NFL in total yards from scrimmage...recorded his first career receptions in 1997, finishing the year with three catches for 33 yards...his versatility on special teams has proven to be an added bonus...led all offensive players and was third on the team with 20 special teams tackles in 1997...has 53 special teams tackles in three NFL seasons.

Receiving	No.	Yards	Avg.	Long	TD
1997	3	33	11.0	12	0

COWBOYS

jason garrett

6-2 ★ 195
BORN: 3/28/66 ★ CHAGRIN, OH
PRINCETON ★ 6TH SEASON
FREE AGENT FOR 1993

QUARTERBACK

After going undrafted in 1989, now enters his sixth season on the Cowboys roster...of the 16 quarterbacks drafted in 1989, only two (Troy Aikman and Rodney Peete) were on NFL rosters in 1997...enters 1997 season as the back-up to Aikman...inactive as the third quarterback in 15-of-16 regular season games in 1997...saw fourth quarter action in season finale against the N.Y. Giants and was 10-of-14 for 56 yards...last NFL start came on Thanksgiving Day 1994 against Green Bay when he orchestrated a 42-31 come-from-behind victory with 36-second half points (a club record)...finished the day 15-of-26 for 311 yards, two touchdowns...prior to joining Dallas had stints with the San Antonio Riders of the World League (1991-92) and the Ottawa RoughRiders of the Canadian Football League (1991)...originally signed with the Saints after a college career at Princeton where he was named the 1988 Ivy League Player of the Year.

Passing	Att.	Comp.	Yards	Pct.	TD	Int	Long	Sks/Yds	Rating
1997	14	10	56	71.4	0	0	12	2/18	78.3
Career	72	42	522	58.3	3	1	68	5/37	89.0

COWBOYS

46

randall godfrey

6-2 ★ 237
BORN: 4/6/73 ★ VALDOSTA, GA
GEORGIA ★ 3rd SEASON
D2b FOR 1996

LINEBACKER

When the Dallas Cowboys drafted Randall Godfrey in 1996, they were looking for an aggressive linebacker that could provide depth in the linebacking corps and contribute on special teams...earned the starting strongside linebacker job midway through his rookie season...followed up a successful rookie season with an even better second year, recording 149 tackles (second on the team) and seven tackles for losses...led the team in tackles five times in 1997...led the team with a career-high 14 tackles, two quarterback pressures and a tackle for a loss against Arizona (11/9/97)...tied his career-high with 14 tackles against Carolina (12/8/97)...became the first rookie to earn a regular starting job on defense since Darrin Smith in 1993 and the first rookie to start at strongside linebacker since Randy Shannon in 1989...four year starter at linebacker for Georgia...preseason All-America as a senior...second on team with 102 tackles as a junior.

COWBOYS

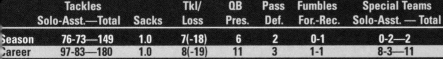

	Tackles Solo-Asst.—Total	Sacks	Tkl/ Loss	QB Pres.	Pass Def.	Fumbles For.-Rec.	Special Teams Solo-Asst. — Total
Season	76-73—149	1.0	7(-18)	6	2	0-1	0-2—2
Career	97-83—180	1.0	8(-19)	11	3	1-1	8-3—11

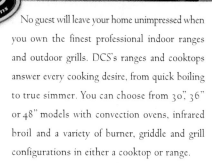

toby gowin

5-10 ★ 167
BORN: 3/30/75
JACKSONVILLE, TX
NORTH TEXAS ★ 2ND SEASON
FA FOR 1997

PUNTER

With the departure of John Jett in free agency in 1997, the Cowboys were in need of a dependable, consistent punter to step into action. Cowboys' kicking coach Steve Hoffman once again found just the player Dallas needed in Toby Gowin...only the fourth Dallas punter since 1984...stepped into the spotlight as a rookie free agent at training camp and did not disappoint...averaged almost 41 yards-per-punt throughout his collegiate career at the University of North Texas...established a Dallas rookie record for punts in a season with 86, breaking Mike Saxon's rookie mark of 81 set in 1985 and tying Saxon's club record for punts in a season set in 1986...at 41.8 yards-per-punt, posted the third highest average by a rookie punter in Dallas history...established a club record by averaging 55.3 yards-per-punt (six punts for 332 yards) against Chicago (9/28/97), topping the mark of 53.4 set by Ron Widby against New Orleans on Nov. 3, 1968.

Punting	No.	Yards	Avg.	Long	TB	IN20	Blk.	Ret.	Ret. Yds.	Net
Season	86	3,592	41.8	72	9	26	0	40	365	35.4

COWBOYS

49

dale hellestrae

6-5 ★ 291 ★ BORN: 7/11/62
SCOTTSDALE, AZ
SOUTHERN METHODIST
14TH SEASON
TRADE (RAIDERS) 1990

GUARD/CENTER

The one task nobody notices as long as everything goes smoothly is the job of deep snapper, and for the past eight seasons Dale Hellestrae, who handles all of the Dallas deep snapping chores on punts and kicks, has quietly gone about his work without drawing attention to himself, which means things are going well for the kicking game...special teams have played a major role in Dallas' rise to the top of the NFL, and Hellestrae has been an important figure in that success...came to Dallas in 1990 in a trade with the L.A. Raiders...Cowboys have not had a punt blocked or a snap fumbled in 545 regular-season punts, and they have not had a fumbled snap in 294 field goal attempts...Dale and his wife Brooke have two daughters, Hillary and Kendyll.

1996 GAMES/STARTS:	16/0
CAREER GAMES/STARTS:	156/2

COWBOYS

50

chad hennings

6-6 ★ 291 ★ BORN: 10/20/65
ELBERON, IA
AIR FORCE ★ 7TH SEASON
D-11 FOR 1988

DEFENSIVE TACKLE

Chad Hennings has shown the NFL why Dallas was willing to wait for his run stuffing abilities after drafting him in the 11th round of the 1988 NFL draft...in six seasons with the team, the Dallas defense has finished as one of the top three units in the league four times and has never finished below 10th...over the last four seasons ranks behind only Pro Bowl defensive end Tony Tolbert among defensive linemen in tackles (48.3 per season), quarterback pressures (21.3) and sacks (5.5)...recovered a Kent Graham fumble and returned in four yards for a touchdown at Arizona (9/7/97), his first career touchdown....went from active duty in the U.S. Air Force — after serving in Desert Storm — to three Super Bowl titles in five years with Dallas...served four years of his military commitment before having his obligation cut short by the government.

	Tackles Solo-Asst.—Total	Sacks	Tkl/ Loss	QB Pres.	Int	Pass Def.	Fumbles For.-Rec.	Blk.
Season	25-27—52	4.5	2(-6)	6		1	0-1	
Career	122-91—213	22.0	11(-27)	90		6	3-4	1

COWBOYS

51

tony hutson

6-3 ★ 313 ★ BORN: 3/13/74
HOUSTON, TX
NORTHEASTERN OKLAHOMA
STATE ★ 2ND SEASON
FA FOR 1997

GUARD/TACKLE

Enters the 1998 season as one of the team's top backups at both the tackle and guard positions, which is a long way from where Hutson was just prior to the NFL Draft in 1996 when he had a benign tumor removed from his lung, a condition that prevented him from being drafted... signed as a free agent with the Cowboys, and competed for a roster spot as a rookie...won himself a roster spot midway through the 1997 season...saw his first NFL action at right tackle for Erik Williams for three plays against Arizona (11/9)...against Washington (11/16), in just his second NFL game, earned his first career start, replacing Williams, who was still bothered by the sprained right ankle, at right tackle...was part of a unit that allowed just one sack in 46 pass plays as Dallas posted a 17-14 come-from-behind win over the Redskins... NAIA All-America at Northeastern Oklahoma State.

1997 GAMES/STARTS:	5/1
CAREER GAMES/STARTS:	5/1

COWBOYS

We can't predict the future, but we
can show you
the best way to experience it.

The new line of Compaq Presario home PCs and printers is here.

And so is the future. Want to link up with the latest DVD, digital

VCR and digital camcorder technology? No problem. The next gen-

eration of flat panel monitors? We're prepared. The smoothest, most

personalized Internet experience? Consider it done. Fully inte-

grated notebooks? You're looking

at them. Need to store lots of

data on disks you can remove?

You'll find a 100 MB Iomega Zip

Built-In™ drive.* And don't forget,

everything's backed up by the most comprehensive customer service

around. So if you want the best value and performance in home com-

puting, what are you waiting for? With the addition of our new line

of printers, we now have the complete solution. **Which means it's**

time to bring the world's best-selling computers home today.

Available at Office Depot.

The new Compaq Presario 1200, 1600, 2250, 5000, 5100 and 5600 Series and color inkjet printers.

Taking Care Of Business

michael irvin

6-2 ★ 207 ★ BORN 3/5/66
FT. LAUDERDALE, FL
MIAMI (FL) ★ 11TH SEASON
D-1 FOR 1988

WIDE RECEIVER

With each pass reception and receiving yard he gains, Michael Irvin adds to his Dallas Cowboys records for career receptions (currently 666), yardage (10,680) and consecutive games with a reception (108)...owns or shares 20 Cowboys receiving records, including nearly every major career or single-season standard...dating back to Dec. 30, 1990, Irvin has at least one catch in each of the Cowboys' last 108 regular season games...only Dallas receiver to be selected to five Pro Bowls (1991-95)...currently 11th in NFL history in receptions and 12th in league history in receiving yardage...has led the team in receptions for seven consecutive seasons...has led or tied for the team lead in catches in 73 of the past 110 regular season games...has a catch of 20-yards-or-more in 110 of the 154 NFL games he has played...has a club-record 43 career 100-yard receiving games...has six career 100-yard receiving days in the postseason, one shy of the NFL record of seven by Jerry Rice...also has 83 post-season receptions, second in NFL history.

Receiving	No.	Yards	Avg.	Long	TD
Season	75	1,180	15.7	55	9
Career	666	10,680	16.0	87t	61

COWBOYS

daryl johnston

6-2 ★ 242 ★ BORN: 2/10/66
YOUNGSTOWN, NY ★ SYRACUSE
10TH SEASON ★ D-2 FOR 1989

FULLBACK

Long respected by teammates for his contribution to the Dallas offense, Daryl "Moose" Johnston has proven himself to be a tireless competitor and team player...it took nine seasons before a neck injury finally forced him out of the lineup for the first time in his NFL career...had never missed a game in his NFL career - playing in 149 straight, including playoffs, before sitting out a game against Jacksonville on Oct. 19, 1997...underwent a successful neck operation in October and declared that he would return to the field in 1998...over the past eight seasons as a lead blocker, has helped guide Emmitt Smith to 11,234 rushing yards — including seven straight 1,000 yards rushing seasons, six Pro Bowl appearances and four NFL rushing titles... has hauled in 275 passes for 2,163 yards and 13 touchdowns in his career...the 275 receptions represent the third highest total by a running back in team history

Rushing	Att.	Yards	Avg.	Long	TD	Receiving	No.	Yards	Avg.	Long	TD
Season	2	3	1.5	3	0	Season	18	166	9.2	21	1
Career	224	736	3.2	18	8	Career	275	2,163	7.9	28	13

COWBOYS

55

When it comes to paper,
there's only one champion.

We're proud that the Dallas Cowboys Yearbook is printed on Champion papers. Champion is one of America's leading manufacturers of paper for business communications, commercial printing and publications, as well as a major producer of plywood and lumber.

 **Champion**
Champion International Corporation

david lafleur

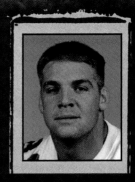

6-7 ★ 280 ★ BORN: 1/29/74,
WESTLAKE, LA ★ LSU
2ND SEASON ★ D-1 FOR 1997

TIGHT END

The prototypical tight end, who can open holes for the running game and catch passes in traffic…recorded 18 catches for 122 yards and two touchdowns while helping open holes for the running game…his 18 receptions were the second highest reception total by a rookie tight end in Cowboys history (Billy Joe DuPree, 29 in 1973), and his two touchdown catches tied for the third highest touchdown total by a rookie tight end in team history…started three of the final four games of the season…registered three receptions for 29 yards, including two touchdown catches, at Cincinnati (12/14)…that effort marked the first time a Dallas tight end had recorded multiple touchdown catches in a game since Jay Novacek scored twice at Washington on Dec. 13, 1992…the 22nd selection in the NFL Draft, is the first LSU Tiger to be drafted by Dallas…a consensus All-SEC first-team selection and a member of the Walter Camp All-America Team.

RECEIVING

Year	No.	Yds.	Avg.	Long	TD
1997	18	122	6.8	17	2

COWBOYS

leon lett

6-6 ★ 295 ★ BORN: 10/12/68
FAIRHOPE, AL
EMPORIA STATE ★ 8TH SEASON
D-7 FOR 1991

DEFENSIVE TACKLE

Originally an unheralded seventh-round draft choice from tiny Emporia State in Kansas, has succeeded in earning a spot in the starting lineup, and an invitation to the Pro Bowl (1994)...has since taken full advantage of his playing time as one of the league's top young defensive tackles...nicknamed "Big Cat" by teammates for his agility, has evolved into a powerful run stuffer and speedy pass rusher...had seven tackles, two quarterback pressures, a pass defensed and a tackle for a loss against Carolina (12/8/97)...was a key part of a Dallas defense that finished the 1996 season ranked third in the NFL...in six consecutive games from Week Four through Nine he recorded a tackle behind the line of scrimmage...despite missing the final three games of the regular season he led the team with seven tackles for a loss in 1996...tied for the team lead with a career-high three forced fumbles.

	Tackles Solo-Asst.—Total	Sacks	Tkl/ Loss	QB Pres.	Int	Pass Def.	Fumbles For.-Rec.	Blk.
Season	9-6—15	0.5	2(-2)	2		1		
Career	141-109—250	14.5	26(-53)	97		18	5-5	4

COWBOYS

kevin mathis

5-9 ★ 172
BORN: 4/29/74 ★ GAINSVILLE, TX
TEXAS A&M-COMMERCE
2ND SEASON ★ FA FOR 1997

CORNERBACK

Kevin Mathis earned his entry into the NFL the hard way, by making a Cowboys team that had no shortage of quality defensive backs as an undrafted rookie free agent...finished the preseason by leading the NFL in interceptions with three, one of which he returned 27 yards for a touchdown...was one of three rookie free agents to play the entire 1997 season for the Cowboys...started the final three games at cornerback following Deion Sandersi season ending rib fracture...finished the season ranked fourth on the squad with 16 kicking game tackles...earned a special teams game ball for his play against Philadelphia (9/15), leading the team with three special teams tackles...led the Cowboys in special teams tackles against Washington (three on 11/16) and at Green Bay (three on 11/23)...earned his first NFL start against Carolina (12/8) and responded with three tackles and three passes defensed, the most passes defensed in a game by a rookie since Larry Brown had four against Houston (11/10/91).

	Tackles Solo-Asst.—Total	Pass Def.	Fumbles For.-Rec.	Special Teams Solo-Asst. — Total
Season	16-7—23	5	1-1	9-7—16

PUNT RETURNS

Year	No.	Yds.	Avg.	Long	TD
1997	11	91	8.3	45	0

burvin McCORMACK

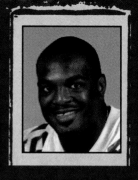

6-5 ★ 284
BORN 4/6/72 ★ BROOKLYN, NY
INDIANA ★ 5th SEASON

DEFENSIVE LINE

A versatile talent on the defensive line—an area where NFL caliber performers are very difficult to find...came to the Cowboys as an unheralded and underrated talent out of Indiana, and he went on to earn a 1994 roster spot based on a very impressive showing in his rookie training camp...has worked his way into the role of a solid contributor in the Cowboys defensive line rotation...finished his fourth pro season third on the team with eight quarterback pressures...led all defensive linemen with three tackles at Washington (10/13)...earned a game ball with three tackles against Jacksonville (10/19), while helping hold the Jaguars to just 42 yards rushing on 18 carries (2.3 avg.)...has played in 49 of the past 53 games for Dallas...earned four starts in 1996, three at right defensive end and one at right defensive tackle...member of Cowboys Super Bowl XXX championship team.

	Tackles Solo-Asst.—Total	Sacks	Tkl/ Loss	QB Pres.	Pass Int	Fumbles Def.	For.-Rec.
Season	9-10—19	0.5	1(-1)	8			
Career	35-27—62	5.0	5(-10)	29			1-0

COWBOYS

"Mind doing that again? I was changing my battery." Only Sony Handycam® camcorders allow you to record with a 12-hour battery.* And along with this added stamina, you'll also get up-to-the-minute battery life readings. So you'll always know exactly how much recording time you have left. Because no moment is going to repeat itself. No matter how politely you ask.

SONY

www.sony.com/handycam

everett mcIver

6-5 ★ 318
BORN 8/5/70 ★ FAYETTEVILLE, N
ELIZABETH CITY STATE
5TH SEASON
UFA (MIA) FOR 1998

GUARD

After four years learning the skills needed to play on the offensive line in the NFL, Everett McIver blossomed into a full-time starter with the Dolphins in 1997...started 19 of the 21 games with Miami in 1996-97...was a key part of a line that helped running back Karim Abdul-Jabbar post back-to-back double figure rushing touchdown totals the last two seasons...Abdul-Jabbar was second in the NFL in rushing touchdowns over the past two seasons with 26...helped the Dolphins post a 9-7 record in 1997 and return to the playoffs...helped spring Abdul-Jabbar for 15 rushing touchdowns on the season, a Dolphins single-season record and a share of the NFL lead...offensive line yielded just 22 sacks on the season, second fewest in the NFL, and had seven games without allowing a sack...spent spring of 1996 with the London Monarchs of NFL Europe...spent the 1993 season on the Cowboys practice squad before joining the N.Y. Jets in 1994.

1997 GAMES/STARTS:	14/14
CAREER GAMES/STARTS:	37/23

COWBOYS

ernie mills

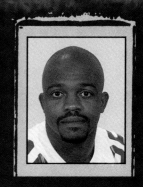

5-11 ★ 192
BORN 10/28/68 ★ DUNNELLON, FL
FLORIDA ★ 8TH SEASON
FA FOR 1998

WIDE RECEIVER

Ernie Mills not only brings seven years of NFL experience to Dallas, but he also brings a familiarity of new head coach Chan Gailey's offense...worked under Gailey in Pittsburgh from 1994-96...established career-highs for receptions (39), receiving yards (679) and touchdowns (8) in 1995...signed with the Cowboys as a free agent on Feb. 27 after being released by Carolina following the 1997 season...against St. Louis (12/20), led the team with five catches for 66 yards and a touchdown...in Super Bowl XXX against Dallas (1/28/96), was the game's leading receiver with eight receptions for 78 yards before tearing the anterior cruciate ligament in his left knee during the fourth quarter...spent a good deal of 1996 recovering from the torn ACL from the Super Bowl.

RECEIVING

Year	No.	Yds.	Avg.	Long	TD
Season	11	127	11.5	37	1
Career	138	2,130	15.4	62t	16

COWBOYS

63

singor mobley

5-11 ★ 195
BORN 10/12/72 ★ TACOMA, WA
WASHINGTON STATE
2ND SEASON ★ FA FOR 1997

SAFETY

Signed as a free agent last season, Singor Mobley provides the Cowboys depth at safety and on special teams...one of three rookie free agents to make the team in 1997...a big hitter, provided the defense with additional run support and came into his own as a special teams player the second half of his rookie season...had two years of professional football experience from the pass-happy Canadian Football League as a member of the Edmonton Eskimos...saw action in each of the final 11 games...went on to record a special teams tackle in eight of the final 10 games of the season and finished seventh on the team with 11 special teams tackles...finished his second CFL season with the Edmonton Eskimos with 72 tackles, five sacks, an interception and a fumble recovery...tallied two tackles against Toronto in a 43-37 loss in the Grey Cup...honorable mention All-Pac 10 selection at Washington State while playing for Cowboys secondary coach Mike Zimmer.

COWBOYS

	Tackles Solo-Asst.—Total	Special Teams Solo-Asst. — Total
Season	0-2—2	5-6—11

64

nate **newton**

6-3 ★ 320
BORN 12/20/61 ★ ORLANDO, FL
FLORIDA A & M ★ 13TH SEASON
FREE AGENT FOR 1986

GUARD

Began his professional career as a free agent signee of the Washington Redskins who was released on the final cut of the 1983 summer training camp...after playing two seasons in the USFL, joined Cowboys in 1986...suffered through two of the worst seasons in Dallas Cowboys franchise history before going on to win three Super Bowl titles as a starter on the Dallas offensive line...enters his 12th year as a starter...for a good portion of his career, he has been regarded as one of the NFL's very best offensive guards...member of the NFC Pro Bowl squad in five of the past six seasons...has started 92 of the Cowboys last 96 regular season games at left guard...has started more regular season games on the Dallas offensive line (164) than any other current Cowboy...has played a prominent role on an offensive line that has allowed just 96 sacks in 64 games over the last four season, fewest in the NFL.

1997 GAMES/STARTS:	13/13
CAREER:	175/164

COWBOYS

jimmy oliver

5-10 ★ 186
BORN: 1/30/73 ★ DALLAS, TX
TEXAS CHRISTIAN
3RD SEASON ★ FA FOR 1998

WIDE RECEIVER

The Dallas Cowboys hope they have captured lighting in a bottle with wide receiver Jimmy Oliver, a two-year starter and two-time All-America sprinter at Texas Christian University...an athletic receiver with world-class speed, the former track star has the excellent hands and body control needed to compete for playing time in the NFL...joins the Cowboys in 1998 as a free agent after two injury plagued seasons with the San Diego Chargers...was originally a second-round draft choice in 1995 and the 61st player taken overall in that draft...sat out 1996 and 1997 seasons after knee surgeries...had rookie season cut short with a dislocated right shoulder in San Diego's first preseason game...started 24-of-39 games at wide receiver for Texas Christian University, recording 55 receptions for 1,058 yards (19.2 avg.) and 11 touchdowns...Was also a two-time All-America selection as a member of the Horned Frogs' 4x100-meter relay team.

COWBOYS

66

kavika pittman

6-6 ★ 267 ★ BORN: 2/9/74
LEESVILLE, LA
McNEESE STATE ★ 3RD SEASON
D-2A FOR 1996

DEFENSIVE END

Three years ago, Kavika Pittman was dominating collegiate football on the I-AA level and today, he is battling for a starting defensive end position with the Dallas Cowboys...spent the first two years of his professional career adding strength and quickness while learning the intricacies of playing defensive end in the NFL from Pro Bowl ends Tony Tolbert and Charles Haley...registered the best statistical game of his professional career with extensive playing time in the season finale against the N.Y. Giants (12/21), totaling four tackles, two tackles for losses, a quarterback pressure and his first career sack...finished his rookie season third on the team with 17 special teams tackles - tops among rookies...drafted 37th overall, was the first McNeese State player ever drafted by Dallas...was the Louisiana and Southland Conference Defensive Player of the Year and earned All-America honors following his senior season.

COWBOYS

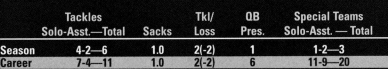

	Tackles Solo-Asst.—Total	Sacks	Tkl/ Loss	QB Pres.	Special Teams Solo-Asst. — Total
Season	4-2—6	1.0	2(-2)	1	1-2—3
Career	7-4—11	1.0	2(-2)	6	11-9—20

deion sanders

6-1 ★ 195
BORN: 8/9/67 ★ FORT MYERS, FL
FLORIDA STATE
10TH SEASON
FA (SAN FRANCISCO) FOR '95

CORNERBACK
WIDE RECEIVER

On Sept. 9, 1995, the Dallas Cowboys signed Deion Sanders, one of the most talented players to ever play the game of football...a standout cornerback, Sanders is also a dangerous kickoff and punt returner as well as a threat at wide receiver...only man in professional sports history to play in both a World Series and in the Super Bowl...became the NFL's first two-way starter since Chuck Bednarik in 1962 when he lined up at wide receiver and cornerback for Dallas in 1996...only man in NFL history who has recorded both a pass reception — a 47-yarder in Super Bowl XXX - and an interception - returned for 15 yards in Super Bowl XXIX - in Super Bowl action....holds the NFL record for career touchdowns scored on any type of return with 14 (TDs have come on seven interceptions, three kickoff returns, three punt returns and one fumble return)...earned his sixth Pro Bowl selection at cornerback following the 1997 season.

	Tackles Solo-Asst.—Total	Sacks	Tkl/ Loss	QB Pres.	Int	Pass Def.	Fumbles For.-Rec.
Season	20-9—29		1(-1)		2	10	
Career	274-103—377	1.0	3(-7)	1	36	106	8-4

Kickoff Ret.	Att.	Yards	Avg.	Long	TD
Season	1	18	18.0	18	0
Career	148	3,403	23.0	100t	3

Punt Returns	No.	FC	Yards	Avg.	Long	TD
Season	33	12	407	12.3	83t	1
Career	128	53	1,254	9.8	83t	3

steve Scifres

6-4 ★ 300 ★ BORN: 1/22/72
COLORADO SPRINGS, CO
WYOMING ★ 2ND SEASON
D-3b FOR 1997

OFFENSIVE LINE

A promising young talent who has an opportunity to compete for playing time on the Cowboys offensive line this year... Scifres (pronounced SIGH-furs) is a hard working player who is also quite versatile, allowing him to fight for playing time at center, guard and tackle in 1998...one of nine rookie draft choices from the class of '97 to make the Cowboys roster (third round 83rd overall)...saw action at every offensive line position, but mostly served as a back-up at tackle throughout his rookie season...started every game of his college career at Wyoming—47 straight...permitted just four sacks on 1,216 passing plays throughout his career...one of 13 semi-finalists for the Outland trophy, while also earning All-America honors...team captain during a senior year in which the Cowboys finished the season ranked third nationally in total offense and first in passing offense...was named All-Western Athletic Conference three straight years...honorable mention All-America as a junior.

COWBOYS

NIKE

Finally, a football line with some real muscle behind it.

Introducing the Official Football of the NFL PLAYERS by Spalding

Here's the line of footballs the NFL PLAYERS play when they're not working. Spalding is endorsed by the guys who know more than a little bit about the game – the NFL PLAYERS.

When the helmets come off and these guys hit the backyard gridirons, Spalding is the only football they play. What are you playing?

SPALDING
The Official Ball of the NFL PLAYERS

PLAYERS INC

clay shiver

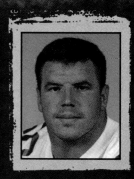

6-2 ★ 294 ★ BORN: 12/7/72
TIFTON, GA ★ FLORIDA STATE
2ND SEASON ★ D-3a FOR 1996

CENTER

In 1997, Clay Shiver stepped into the starting center position for the Dallas Cowboys, and in doing so, he shouldered the responsibility of a solid tradition of outstanding performances from the men who handled that spot in the past…gained his introduction into the intricacies of making the calls at the line of scrimmage for Dallas in just his second year as a professional player in 1997… follows a long line of great centers in Dallas: John Fitzgerald (1973-1980), Tom Rafferty (1981-1989), Mark Stepnoski (1990-1994) and Ray Donaldson (1994-1995)…position holds the heritage of protecting the likes of Roger Staubach, Danny White and Troy Aikman…has displayed the credentials to create optimism for the Cowboys offense following his first season at center…in first NFL start, helped Dallas gain 380 total yards, 295 passing, at Pittsburgh (8/31) while holding the Steelers without a sack… played a key role in allowing just one sack in 46 passing plays in the come-from-behind victory over the Redskins (11/16).

1997 GAMES/STARTS:	16/16
CAREER:	30/16

COWBOYS

emmitt smith

5-9 ★ 209 ★ BORN: 5/15/69
ESCAMBIA, FL
FLORIDA ★ 9TH SEASON
D-1 FOR 1990

RUNNING BACK

In his eight seasons in Dallas, Emmitt Smith has garnered almost every award imaginable for a running back...four times (1991, 1992, 1993 and 1995) he has led the NFL in rushing...established a NFL record in 1995 with 25 touchdowns...also became the first non-kicker to lead the league in scoring (150 points) since Jerry Rice in 1987...in 1997 became the fourth player in NFL history to rush for over 1,000 yards in seven consecutive seasons... first player in NFL history with five consecutive seasons with over 1,400 yards rushing...second in NFL history with 112 career rushing touchdowns...a six-time Pro Bowler...including playoffs, Dallas is 75-12 when Smith carries 20-or-more times, 46-9 when he rushes for 100 yards...is 11th in NFL history with 11,234 yards rushing in his career...with 119 career TDs is fifth on the NFL's all-time TD list...the only non-kicker in Dallas history to top the 100 point plateau in a season.

Rushing	Att.	Yards	Avg.	Long	TD	Receiving	No.	Yards	Avg.	Long	TD
Season	261	1,074	4.1	44	4	Season	40	234	5.9	24	0
Career	2,595	11,234	4.3	75t	112	Career	388	2,434	6.3	86	7

BREITLING
1884

CHRONOMAT GT

Developed in tandem with Italy's crack *Frecce Tricolori* aerobatics team, the CHRONOMAT is now available in a GT (for Grand Totalizer) version, with its unmistakable precision-instrument dial face.

Of all selfwinding chronographs, the CHRONOMAT is surely the most universally popular, cutting through time at will to capture and measure the instant as efficiently as the fabled delta-winged *Concorde*.

deBoulle
214.522.2400

Mechanical chronograph

Designed for the implacable world of air combat, the CHRONOMAT counts and displays all time spans from 1/5th of a second to 12 hours, providing intermediate and cumulative flying times. Its rider-tab rotating bezel also doubles as a practical, at-a-glance visual guide.

Water-resistant to 100 m (330 feet), its case comes in steel, two-tone finish, steel and gold or solid 18 K yellow or white gold, fitted with the BREITLING bracelet of your choice.

For a Breitling catalog,
please call 1.800.641.7343

INSTRUMENTS FOR PROFESSIONALS™

kevin smith

5-11 ★ 190
BORN: 4/7/70 ★ ORANGE, TX
TEXAS A&M ★ 7TH SEASON
D-1a FOR 1992

CORNERBACK

Production and results are what have characterized Kevin Smith's Dallas career since the day he was drafted in the first round (17th overall) out of Texas A&M in 1992...took over the starting corner position 10 games into his rookie season and started Super Bowl XXVII as a 22-year old rookie...set a career-high with 17 passes defensed in 1994...returned from a ruptured right Achilles tendon suffered in 1995 to establish a new career-high with 18 passes defensed in 1996...has led the Cowboys in passes defensed every year he's been in the league, except his rookie season and 1995 when he was injured...currently has 16 career interceptions, which is more than any current Cowboy player has collected while wearing a Dallas uniform...with fellow corner Deion Sanders, Smith makes up one half of what many believe to be the best pair of cornerbacks in the NFL...selected to receive the 1996 Ed Block Courage Award.

	Tackles Solo-Asst. — Total	Tkl/ Loss	Int	Pass Def.	Fumbles For.-Rec.	Special Teams Solo-Asst. — Total
Season	37-9—46	1(-2)	1	13	2-0	
Career	240-60—300	1(-2)	15	68	6-1	4-1—5

COWBOYS

75

omar stoutmire

5-11 ★ 198
BORN: 7/9/74 ★ LONG BEACH, CA
FRESNO STATE
2ND SEASON ★ D-7 FOR 1997

SAFETY

When the Cowboys drafted Omar Stoutmire in the seventh round (224th overall) of the 1997 draft, they were looking for a player that could provide depth in the secondary and contribute on special teams...provided that and more as he finished sixth on the team with 76 tackles to lead all non-starters...play in the secondary helped the Cowboys finish the year with the top ranked pass unit in the NFL...76 tackles placed him seventh in the NFL among rookies and led all Cowboy non-starters...two sacks were the most by a Dallas rookie since Russell Maryland had 4.5 in 1991...recorded three tackles and a fourth quarter sack in the season opener at Pittsburgh (8/31/97), the first sack by a Dallas rookie since Darrin Smith recorded one against San Francisco on Oct. 17, 1993...earned his first NFL start at Philadelphia (10/26/97) for an injured Darren Woodson and totaled 13 tackles... posted a career-high 16 tackles against Tennessee (11/27/97).

COWBOYS

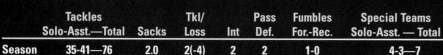

	Tackles Solo-Asst.—Total	Sacks	Tkl/ Loss	Int	Pass Def.	Fumbles For.-Rec.	Special Teams Solo-Asst. — Total
Season	35-41—76	2.0	2(-4)	2	2	1-0	4-3—7

fred strickland

6-2 ★ 251
BORN: 8/15/66 ★ WANAQUE, NJ
PURDUE ★ 11TH SEASON

LINEBACKER

Fred Strickland's experience and run stopping ability have made him a valuable acquisition for the Cowboys since coming to Dallas as an unrestricted free agent on March 11, 1996…has stepped into the starting middle linebacker role for the Cowboys the past two years and posted 285 tackles, including a career-high 153 stops in 1996…provides veteran leadership and an aggressive style of play…had double figures in tackles in six of the final nine games of the 1997 season…logged a season-high 15 tackles in leading the team at Philadelphia (10/26/97)…his 153 tackles in 1996 was the 12th best total in the NFL…came to Dallas after two seasons with Green Bay, where he started 24 of his 30 regular-season games and helped the Packers reach the 1995 NFC Championship Game…in each of the last five seasons, has been the starting middle linebacker on a defense that ranked in the top 14 in the NFL in overall defense.

	Tackles Solo-Asst.—Total	Sacks	Tkl/ Loss	QB Pres.	Int	Pass Def.	Fumbles For.-Rec.	Special Teams Solo-Asst.—Total
Season	71-61—132	0.5	3(-6)	5		3	1-2	
Career	473-276—749	8.5	11.5	13	4	23	5-9	19-2—21

COWBOYS

77

nicky SUALUA

5-11 ★ 257 ★ BORN: 4/16/75
SANTA ANA, CA
OHIO STATE ★ 2ND SEASON
D-4c FOR 1997

FULLBACK

For several years, the Cowboys have been searching for a powerful blocker to back-up Daryl Johnston at fullback. With the arrival of Nicky Sualua, one of the most physical and aggressive blockers in the college game, Dallas hopes to have filled that role…built his reputation with the work he does for the ball carrier, not as the ball carrier…a battering ram of a player at 5-11, 257-pounds…a tough, hard-nosed blocker who eagerly leads the charge up the middle…saw his first NFL action as the back-up fullback behind the promoted Herschel Walker against Jacksonville (10/19)…one of three fourth-round draft choices by Dallas (129th overall) and one of seven Buckeyes taken in the 1997 NFL Draft…averaged 5.5 yards-per-carry for his college career on teams that amassed a 20-6 record while he was in the lineup… blocking was a big part of Eddie George's Heisman Trophy winning season at Ohio State in 1995.

COWBOYS

Beyond Ordinary, Close to Perfection.

Minutes from where you need to be, here is where you want to be.
A gated, limited-access, masterplanned community with wooded creeks, century-old Spanish Oaks, recreation center and exclusive neighborhood living.

Featuring new custom estate homesites from 1/3 to 1 acre+.
Chamberlyne Place and Chamberlyne Place Estates!

HOMES FROM THE ★ $300s - $1MILLION+

TM

HOURS:
10 - 6 Mon. - Sat.
12 - 6 Sunday
Drive North on Dallas
Tollway, 2 miles North of
SH121, turn left on Lebanon
Road to the Starwood
Community Center

(972) 335-6800

LEBANON

2 miles

HWY 121

TOLLWAY

PRESTON RD.

N

george teague

6-1 ★ 196 ★ BORN: 2/18/71
MONTGOMERY, AL
ALABAMA ★ 6TH SEASON
FA FOR 1998

SAFETY

George Teague made his return to the Dallas Cowboys when he signed as a free agent on May 6 after being released by the Miami Dolphins...brings to the Cowboys experience and big-play ability, which he demonstrated as a member of the secondary in Dallas in 1996...recorded a career-high four interceptions and 70 tackles, the second highest total of his career, in his first stint in Dallas...turned the tide with Dallas in a playoff game against Minnesota in 1996 by forcing two fumbles and returning an interception for a touchdown...against Detroit in a 1993 playoff game as a member of the Packers, returned an interception 101 yards for a touchdown (the longest in NFL postseason history)...returned an interception 74 yards against Cincinnati in 1995...recorded a season-high 11 tackles and a forced fumble against Chicago (10/27/97) for the Dolphins...preserved Miami's 24-17 victory over the N.Y. Jets (11/9/97) with an interception with 1:15 remaining in the game.

COWBOYS

	Tackles Solo-Asst.—Total	Tkl/ Loss	Int	Pass Def.	Fumbles For.-Rec.
Season	24-19—43	—	2	3	2-0
Career	190-84—274	1(-2)	12	42	4-3

broderick thomas

6-4 ★ 254
BORN: 2/20/67 ★ HOUSTON, TX
NEBRASKA ★ 10TH SEASON
FREE AGENT FOR 1996

DEFENSIVE END/LINEBACKER

Throughout his eight year career, Broderick Thomas has been called upon to put pressure on the opposing quarterback, and he has recorded 47.5 sacks and 44 tackles for losses...the Cowboys have also utilized his pass rushing ability from the defensive end position...led the team in quarterback pressures in 1997 while playing defensive end...finished fourth with three and a half sacks...recorded the 700th tackle of his career during the '97 season...recorded a season-high five tackles and a tackle for a loss against Chicago (9/28)...played in his 162nd consecutive game in the season finale, not having missed a single game in his nine year NFL career...originally drafted by the Buccaneers in 1989 with the sixth overall selection, the third defensive player taken in the draft behind Derrick Thomas (4th) and Deion Sanders (5th)...earned All-America and Big Eight Defensive Player of the Year honors in 1988 at the University of Nebraska.

COWBOYS

	Tackles Solo-Asst.—Total	Sacks	Tkl/ Loss	QB Pres.	Int	Pass Def.	Fumbles For. Rec.
Season	12-19—31	3.5	2(-2)	10		3	0-1
Career	449-280—729	47.5	44	114	2	40	16-15

LOGO ATHLETIC

AUTHENTIC TEAM APPAREL

chris Warren

6-2 ★ 226

BORN: 1/24/68 ★ BURKE, VA

FERRUM ★ 9TH SEASON

FA FOR 1998

RUNNING BACK

After spending the first eight years of his NFL career in Seattle, Chris Warren signed with Dallas on April 13...brings veteran leadership, four 1,000-yard rushing seasons and three Pro Bowl appearances to Dallas...holds six Seattle rushing records, including most yards in a career, most yards in a season, most 100-yard games (career and season) and most touchdowns in a season...a versatile back that has averaged 40 receptions over the last four seasons...also has career averages of 8.7 yards-per-punt return and 20.9 yards-per-kickoff return...finished the 1997 season with 847 rushing yards on 200 carries to surpass Curt Warner (6,705) as the Seahawks all-time leading rusher with 6,706 career yards..also registered a career-high 45 receptions for 257 yards...was the AFC's leading rusher with a team-record 1,545 yards on 333 carries in 1994...also finished second in the NFL in total yards from scrimmage (1,868) and average-per-carry (4.6).

COWBOYS

ushing	Att.	Yards	Avg.	Long	TD	Receiving	No.	Yards	Avg.	Long	TD
eason	200	847	4.2	36t	4	Season	45	257	5.7	20	0
areer	1,559	6,706	4.3	52	44	Career	194	1,342	6.9	51	3

kenny wheaton

5-10 ★ 190
BORN: 3/8/75 ★ PHOENIX, AZ
OREGON ★ 2ND SEASON
D-3c FOR 1997

DEFENSIVE BACK

The Cowboys hope Kenny Wheaton can have some of the success that Mel Renfro, the last defensive back Dallas drafted out of the University of Oregon, had in the NFL...a big-play corner for the Ducks...posted an interception return for a touchdown of 70-or-more yards in each of his three seasons...has the versatility to move between safety and cornerback, a trait that can also be traced back to Renfro...gained 380 yards on interception returns, to break the school's 49-year old record...had the soft hands needed to grab 10 career interceptions in college...but also had the 194 tackles, including a team-high 73 as a senior, needed to defend against the run like a safety...suffered a separated right should against Oakland in the July 31 scrimmage and was slowed the first part of the season...recorded a season-high four tackles against the N.Y. Giants (12/21) while playing cornerback...one of nine rookie draft choices to make the roster.

	Tackles Solo-Asst.—Total	
Season		3-1—4

COWBOYS

charlie williams

6-0 ★ 189
BORN: 2/2/72 ★ DETROIT, MI
BOWLING GREEN
4TH SEASON ★ D3 FOR 1995

SAFETY

Having been a "jack-of-all-trades" player in college, Charlie Williams came to the Cowboys having never settled in at one particular position...because of his athleticism and quickness, Dallas coaches believed his "one position" is as a defensive back...has shown tremendous ability as a special teams player...earned All-Pro honors as a special teams player from *Sports Illustrated*...since returning from knee surgery in 1996, has recorded at least one special teams tackle in 19 of the last 25 games...led Dallas in special teams tackles in 1997 with 26, which placed him seventh in the NFL...recorded a special teams tackle in 14-of-16 games...recorded his first NFL sack against Chicago (9/28)...led the team with three special teams tackles and forced a fumble on a kickoff return at Philadelphia (10/26)...logged his second sack of the season and tallied three special teams tackles against Arizona (11/9)...has successfully returned from a knee injury suffered during the 1996 offseason.

COWBOYS

	Tackles Solo-Asst.—Total	Sacks	QB Pres.	Pass Def.	Fumbles For.-Rec.	Special Teams Solo-Asst. — Total
Season	6-5—11	2.0	3	5	1-0	16-10—26
Career	9-11—20	2.0	2	6	2-0	32-19—51

erik williams

6-6 ★ 328
BORN 9/7/68 ★ PHILADELPHIA, P
CENTRAL STATE (OH.)
8TH SEASON ★ D-3 FOR 1991

TACKLE

A six year starter at right tackle, Erik Williams has evolved into one of the top offensive tackles in the National Football League...has rebounded from a season ending knee injury suffered in mid-1994 to start 50 of the last 51 games for Dallas...earned back-to-back spots in the Pro Bowl in 1996 and 1997...one of the biggest of Dallas' big men in the offensive front at 6-6, 328 pounds...started his sixth season at right tackle in the opener at Pittsburgh (8/31) and helped Dallas gain 380 total yards and 295 yards passing while not allowing a sack...part of a Dallas line that has allowed just 96 sacks over the past four seasons (1994-97), fewest in the NFL...part of a line that has posted the four lowest sacks allowed totals in club history...also part of a unit that led the NFL in 1996 in fewest sacks allowed with 19.

1997 GAMES/STARTS:	15/15
CAREER GAMES/STARTS:	96/88

COWBOYS

GENERATIONNEXT™

BEST BUY and Canon

Always A Winning Combination!
professional tools with a personal touch

PC420

For home office or personal use, offering portability and multiple copying capability, up to 50 letter-size copies.

- Single Cartridge System for virtually maintenance-free performance
- Starter cartridge included
- 4 copies per minute (letter)
- 50-sheet stack tray accepts postcard to letter-size paper
- Makes up to 50 copies at a time
- Instant warm up; no waiting
- Auto shut-off; saves energy
- Warranty – 1-year overnight exchange

PC 745

Affordable copying for the small office providing zoom features, front-loading paper cassette, and no warm-up time.

- Single Cartridge System for virtually maintenance-free performance – cartridge included
- 10 copies per minute (letter); 9 copies per minute (legal)
- Zoom Reduction & Enlargement from 70% to 141% in 1% increments, & four preset ratios
- 250-sheet front-loading paper cassette acccpts statement, letter & legal size paper
- Instant warm up; no waiting
- Makes up to 100 copies at a time
- 3-year warranty - first year on-site

Always Score a Touchdown with Canon Copiers and

sherman Williams

5-8 ★ 202
BORN: 8/13/73 ★ MOBILE, AL
ALABAMA ★ 4TH SEASON
D-2a FOR 1995

RUNNING BACK

The Cowboys search for a reliable back-up for Emmitt Smith ended when they drafted Sherman Williams in the 1995 NFL Draft...a compact back who has powerful legs, great field instincts and catches the ball well...has the explosiveness and break away speed to step into the Dallas lineup and keep the offense moving...has established career highs in rushing attempts and yards, as well as receptions and receiving yards, in each of his first three seasons with the Cowboys...totaled 468 rushing yards in 1997, the most rushing yards by Dallas' second back since Herschel Walker picked up 737 yards in 1986...also had career-highs with 21 receptions and 159 receiving yards...led the team with a career-high seven receptions for a career-high 56 yards against Tennessee (11/27)...set a career-high with 19 carries for a season-best 75 yards against Carolina (12/8)...earned his first NFL start in the 1996 season finale at Washington.

Rushing	Att.	Yards	Avg.	Long	TD	Receiving	No.	Yards	Avg.	Long	TD
Season	121	468	3.9	18	2	Season	21	159	7.6	18	0
Career	238	942	4.0	44t	3	Career	29	228	7.9	24	0

COWBOYS

stepfret williams

6-0 ★ 170
BORN: 6/14/73 ★ MINDEN, LA
NORTHEAST LOUISIANA
3RD SEASON ★ D-3b FOR 1996

WIDE RECEIVER

Although blessed with good speed (4.32 in the 40-yard dash) and hands, Stepfret Williams' work ethic is what made him into the receiver he is today...a dependable clutch player and one of Troy Aikman's "go-to-guys" on third down... has shown the discipline that is necessary to succeed in the NFL... exploded onto the scene on third downs in 1997...led the team with a career-high five receptions for a career-high 53 yards at Arizona (9/7) the second week of the season...went on to record 30 receptions for the season, the best performance by Dallas's third receiver since Kelvin Martin had 32 catches in 1992...19 of his receptions came on third down, the 12th best total in the NFC...15 of his final 22 receptions came on third down and gave Dallas a first down...recorded his first NFL touchdown with a two-yard catch from Troy Aikman against Jacksonville (10/19)...tied his career-high with five receptions for 36 yards at San Francisco (11/2).

Receiving	No.	Yards	Avg.	Long	TD
Season	30	308	10.3	20	1
Career	31	340	11.3	42	1

COWBOYS

$3.00 Music & Video Cash checks, inside specially-marked Sony products!

- Checks are good for $3.00 off the price of any pre-recorded CD, album, audiotape or videotape.
- Immediately redeemable-no rebate form to fill out or mail away.
- Simply present check at the register of any participating retailer.

darren **woodson**

6-1 ★ 219
BORN: 4/25/69 ★ PHOENIX, AZ
ARIZONA STATE ★ 7TH SEASON
D-2b FOR 1992

SAFETY

In each of the past four seasons, Darren Woodson has performed at a level many consider to be the best for strong safeties in the NFL...in six seasons, has played in three Super Bowls, four Pro Bowls and three times has been named first team All-Pro...went over the 100 tackle mark for four consecutive seasons (1993-96), becoming the first Dallas player to accomplish that feat since Michael Downs (1983-86)...in 1995, became the first Dallas defensive back to lead the team in tackles (144) since Bill Bates in 1988...in 1993, established a Dallas single-season record for tackles by a defensive back (155)...a converted college linebacker...is the complete NFL package at safety....combines size (6-1, 219) and speed (4.4 in the 40-yard dash) with great football instincts and hitting ability...versatility makes him a very valuable special teams performer... has started 87 of the last 89 Cowboys games, including playoffs.

	Tackles Solo-Asst.—Total	Sacks	Tkl/ Loss	QB Pres.	Int	Pass Def.	Fumbles For.-Rec.	Special Teams Solo-Asst. — Total
Season	45-52—97	2.0	3(-4)		1	5	3-2	7-2—9
Career	391-269—660	6.0	22(-44)		8	13	43	9-6	55-24—79

COWBOYS

92

Championships

Most Seasons League Champion
- 12 Green Bay, 1929-31, 1936, 1939, 1944, 1961-62, 1965-67, 1996
- 9 Chi. Bears, 1921, 1932-33, 1940-41, 1943, 1946, 1963, 1985
- 6 N.Y. Giants, 1927, 1934, 1938, 1956, 1986, 1990

Most Consecutive Seasons League Champion
- 3 Green Bay, 1929-31
  - Green Bay, 1965-67
- 2 Canton, 1922-23
  - Chi. Bears, 1932-33
  - Chi. Bears, 1940-41
  - Philadelphia, 1948-49
  - Detroit, 1952-53
  - Cleveland, 1954-55
  - Baltimore, 1958-59
  - Houston, 1960-61
  - Green Bay, 1961-62
  - Buffalo, 1964-65
  - Miami, 1972-73
  - Pittsburgh, 1974-75
  - Pittsburgh, 1978-79
  - San Francisco, 1988-89
  - Dallas, 1992-93

Most Times Finishing First, Regular Season
- 19 N.Y. Giants, 1927, 1933-35, 1938-39, 1941, 1944, 1946, 1956, 1958-59, 1961-63, 1986, 1989-90, 1997
- 18 Clev. Browns, 1950-55, 1957, 1964-65, 1967-69, 1971, 1980, 1985-87, 1989
  - Chi. Bears, 1921, 1932-34, 1937, 1940-43, 1946, 1956, 1963, 1984-88, 1990
  - Dallas, 1966-71, 1973, 1976-79, 1981, 1985, 1992-96
- 17 Green Bay, 1929-31, 1936, 1938-39, 1944, 1960-62, 1965-67, 1972, 1995-97

Most Consecutive Times Finishing First, Regular Season
- 7 Los Angeles, 1973-79
- 6 Cleveland, 1950-55
  - Dallas, 1966-71
  - Minnesota, 1973-78
  - Pittsburgh, 1974-79
- 5 Oakland, 1972-76
  - Chicago, 1984-88
  - San Francisco, 1986-90
  - Dallas, 1992-96

Games Won

Most Consecutive Games Won
- 17 Chi. Bears, 1933-34
- 16 Chi. Bears, 1941-42
  - Miami, 1971-73
  - Miami, 1983-84
- 15 L.A. Chargers/San Diego, 1960-61
  - San Francisco, 1989-90

Most Consecutive Games Without Defeat
- 25 Canton, 1921-23 (won 22, tied 3)
- 24 Chi. Bears, 1941-43 (won 23, tied 1)
- 23 Green Bay, 1928-30 (won 21, tied 2)

Most Games Won, Season
- 15 San Francisco, 1984
  - Chicago, 1985
- 14 Frankford, 1926
  - Miami, 1972
  - Pittsburgh, 1978
  - Washington, 1983
  - Miami, 1984
  - Chicago, 1986
  - N.Y. Giants, 1986
  - San Francisco, 1989
  - San Francisco, 1990
  - Washington, 1991
  - San Francisco, 1992
- 13 By many teams

Most Consecutive Games Won, Season
- 14 Miami, 1972
- 13 Chi. Bears, 1934
- 12 Minnesota, 1969
  - Chicago, 1985

Most Consecutive Games Won, Start of Season
- 14 Miami, 1972, entire season
- 13 Chi. Bears, 1934, entire season
- 12 Chicago, 1985

Most Consecutive Games Won, End of Season
- 14 Miami, 1972, entire season
- 13 Chi. Bears, 1934, entire season
- 11 Chi. Bears, 1942, entire season
  - Cleveland, 1951
  - Houston, 1993

Most Consecutive Games Without Defeat, Season
- 14 Miami, 1972 (won 14)
- 13 Chi. Bears, 1926 (won 11, tied 2)
  - Green Bay, 1929 (won 12, tied 1)
  - Chi. Bears, 1934 (won 13)
  - Baltimore, 1967 (won 11, tied 2)
- 12 Canton, 1922 (won 10, tied 2)
  - Canton, 1923 (won 11, tied 1)
  - Minnesota, 1969 (won 12)
  - Chicago, 1985 (won 12)

Most Consecutive Games Without Defeat, Start of Season
- 14 Miami, 1972 (won 14), entire season
- 13 Chi. Bears, 1926 (won 11, tied 2)
  - Green Bay, 1929 (won 12, tied 1), entire season
  - Chi. Bears, 1934 (won 13), entire season
  - Baltimore, 1967 (won 11, tied 2)
- 12 Canton, 1922 (won 10, tied 2), entire season
  - Canton, 1923 (won 11, tied 1), entire season
  - Chicago, 1985 (won 12)

Most Consecutive Games Without Defeat, End of Season
- 14 Miami, 1972 (won 14), entire season
- 13 Green Bay, 1929 (won 12, tied 1), entire season
  - Chi. Bears, 1934 (won 13), entire season
- 12 Canton, 1922 (won 10, tied 2), entire season
  - Canton, 1923 (won 11, tied 1), entire season

Most Consecutive Home Games Won
- 27 Miami, 1971-74
- 23 Green Bay, 1995-97 (current)
- 20 Green Bay, 1929-32

Most Consecutive Home Games Without Defeat
- 30 Green Bay, 1928-33 (won 27, tied 3)
- 27 Miami, 1971-74 (won 27)
- 25 Chi. Bears, 1923-25 (won 19, tied 6)

Most Consecutive Road Games Won
- 18 San Francisco, 1988-90
- 11 L.A. Chargers/San Diego, 1960-61
  - San Francisco, 1987-88
- 10 Chi. Bears, 1941-42
  - Dallas, 1968-69
  - New Orleans, 1987-88

Most Consecutive Road Games Without Defeat
- 18 San Francisco, 1988-90 (won 18)
- 13 Chi. Bears, 1941-43 (won 12, tied 1)
- 12 Green Bay, 1928-30 (won 10, tied 2)

Most Shutout Games Won or Tied, Season
- 10 Pottsville, 1926 (won 9, tied 1)
  - N.Y. Giants, 1927 (won 9, tied 1)
- 9 Akron, 1921 (won 8, tied 1)
  - Canton, 1922 (won 7, tied 2)
  - Frankford, 1926 (won 9)
  - Frankford, 1929 (won 6, tied 3)
- 8 By many teams

Most Consecutive Shutout Games Won or Tied
- 13 Akron, 1920-21 (won 10, tied 3)
- 7 Pottsville, 1926 (won 6, tied 1)
  - Detroit, 1934 (won 7)
- 6 Buffalo, 1920-21 (won 5, tied 1)
  - Frankford, 1926 (won 6)
  - Detroit, 1926 (won 4, tied 2)
  - N.Y. Giants, 1926-27 (won 5, tied 1)

Games Lost

Most Consecutive Games Lost
- 26 Tampa Bay, 1976-77
- 19 Chi. Cardinals, 1942-43, 1945
  - Oakland, 1961-62
- 18 Houston, 1972-73

Most Consecutive Games Without Victory
- 26 Tampa Bay, 1976-77 (lost 26)
- 23 Rochester, 1922-25 (lost 21, tied 2)
  - Washington, 1960-61 (lost 20, tied 3)
- 19 Dayton, 1927-29 (lost 18, tied 1)
  - Chi. Cardinals, 1942-43, 1945 (lost 19)
  - Oakland, 1961-62 (lost 19)

Most Games Lost, Season
- 15 New Orleans, 1980
  - Dallas, 1989
  - New England, 1990
  - Indianapolis, 1991
  - N.Y. Jets, 1996
- 14 By many teams

Most Consecutive Games Lost, Season
14   Tampa Bay, 1976
     New Orleans, 1980
     Baltimore, 1981
     New England, 1990
13   Oakland, 1962
     Pittsburgh, 1969
     Indianapolis, 1986
12   Tampa Bay, 1977

Most Consecutive Games Lost, Start of Season
14   Tampa Bay, 1976, entire season
     New Orleans, 1980
13   Oakland, 1962
     Indianapolis, 1986
12   Tampa Bay, 1977

Most Consecutive Games Lost, End of Season
14   Tampa Bay, 1976, entire season
     New England, 1990
13   Pittsburgh, 1969
11   Philadelphia, 1936
     Detroit, 1942, entire season
     Houston, 1972

Most Consecutive Games Without Victory, Season
14   Tampa Bay, 1976 (lost 14), entire season
     New Orleans, 1980 (lost 14)
     Baltimore, 1981 (lost 14)
     New England, 1990 (lost 14)
13   Washington, 1961 (lost 12, tied 1)
     Oakland, 1962 (lost 13)
     Pittsburgh, 1969 (lost 13)
     Indianapolis, 1986 (lost 13)
12   Dall. Cowboys, 1960 (lost 11, tied 1), entire season
     Tampa Bay, 1977 (lost 12)

Most Consecutive Games Without Victory, Start of Season
14   Tampa Bay, 1976 (lost 14), entire season
     New Orleans, 1980 (lost 14)
13   Washington, 1961 (lost 12, tied 1)
     Oakland, 1962 (lost 13)
     Indianapolis, 1986 (lost 13)
12   Dall. Cowboys, 1960 (lost 11, tied 1), entire season
     Tampa Bay, 1977 (lost 12)

Most Consecutive Games Without Victory, End of Season
14   Tampa Bay, 1976, (lost 14), entire season
     New England, 1990 (lost 14)
13   Pittsburgh, 1969 (lost 13)
12   Dall. Cowboys, 1960 (lost 11, tied 1), entire season

Most Consecutive Home Games Lost
14   Dallas, 1988-89
13   Houston, 1972-73
     Tampa Bay, 1976-77
     N.Y. Jets, 1995-97
11   Oakland, 1961-62
     Los Angeles, 1961-63

Most Consecutive Home Games Without Victory
14   Dallas, 1988-89 (lost 14)
13   Houston, 1972-73 (lost 13)
     Tampa Bay, 1976-77 (lost 13)
     N.Y. Jets, 1995-97 (lost 13)
12   Philadelphia, 1936-38 (lost 11, tied 1)

Most Consecutive Road Games Lost
23   Houston, 1981-84
22   Buffalo, 1983-86
19   Tampa Bay, 1983-85
     Atlanta, 1988-91

Most Consecutive Road Games Without Victory
23   Houston, 1981-84 (lost 23)
22   Buffalo, 1983-86 (lost 22)
19   Tampa Bay, 1983-85 (lost 19)
     Atlanta, 1988-91 (lost 19)

Most Shutout Games Lost or Tied, Season
8   Frankford, 1927 (lost 6, tied 2)
    Brooklyn, 1931 (lost 8)
7   Dayton, 1925 (lost 6, tied 1)
    Orange, 1929 (lost 4, tied 3)
    Frankford, 1931 (lost 6, tied 1)
6   By many teams

Most Consecutive Shutout Games Lost or Tied
8   Rochester, 1922-24 (lost 8)
7   Hammond, 1922-23 (lost 6, tied 1)
6   Providence, 1926-27 (lost 5, tied 1)
    Brooklyn, 1942-43 (lost 6)

Tie Games
Most Tie Games, Season
6   Chi. Bears, 1932

---

5   Frankford, 1929
4   Chi. Bears, 1924
    Orange, 1929
    Portsmouth, 1932

Most Consecutive Tie Games
3   Chi. Bears, 1932
2   By many teams

Scoring
Most Seasons Leading League
10   Chi. Bears, 1932, 1934-35, 1939, 1941-43, 1946-47, 1956
9   San Francisco, 1953, 1965, 1970, 1987, 1989, 1992-95
7   Green Bay, 1931, 1936-38, 1961-62, 1996

Most Consecutive Seasons Leading League
4   San Francisco, 1992-1996
3   Green Bay, 1936-38
    Chi. Bears, 1941-43
    Los Angeles, 1950-52
    Oakland, 1967-69
2   By many teams

Points
Most Points, Season
541   Washington, 1983
513   Houston, 1961
     Miami, 1984
505   San Francisco, 1994

Fewest Points, Season (Since 1932)
37   Cincinnati/St. Louis, 1934
38   Cincinnati, 1933
    Detroit, 1942
51   Pittsburgh, 1934
    Philadelphia, 1936

Most Points, Game
72   Washington vs. N.Y. Giants, Nov. 27, 1966
70   Los Angeles vs. Baltimore, Oct. 22, 1950
65   Chi. Cardinals vs. N.Y. Bulldogs, Nov. 13, 1949
    Los Angeles vs. Detroit, Oct. 29, 1950

Most Points, Both Teams, Game
113   Washington (72) vs. N.Y. Giants (41), Nov. 27, 1966
101   Oakland (52) vs. Houston (49), Dec. 22, 1963
99   Seattle (51) vs. Kansas City (48), Nov. 27, 1983 (OT)

Fewest Points, Both Teams, Game
0   In many games. Last time: N.Y. Giants vs. Detroit, Nov. 7, 1943

Most Points, Shutout Victory, Game
64   Philadelphia vs. Cincinnati, Nov. 6, 1934
62   Akron vs. Oorang, Oct. 29, 1922
60   Rock Island vs. Evansville, Oct. 15, 1922
    Chi. Cardinals vs. Rochester, Oct. 7, 1923

Fewest Points, Shutout Victory, Game
2   Green Bay vs. Chi. Bears, Oct. 16, 1932
    Chi. Bears vs. Green Bay, Sept. 18, 1938

Most Points Overcome to Win Game
28   San Francisco vs. New Orleans, Dec. 7, 1980 (OT) (trailed 7-35, won 38-35)
26   Buffalo vs. Indianapolis, Sept., 21, 1997 (trailed 26-0, won 37-35)
25   St. Louis vs. Tampa Bay, Nov. 8, 1987 (trailed 3-28, won 31-28)

Most Points Overcome to Tie Game
31   Denver vs. Buffalo, Nov. 27, 1960 (trailed 7-38, tied 38-38)
28   Los Angeles vs. Philadelphia, Oct. 3, 1948 (trailed 0-28, tied 28-28)

Most Points, Each Half
1st: 49   Green Bay vs. Tampa Bay, Oct. 2, 1983
     48   Buffalo vs. Miami, Sept. 18, 1966
     45   Green Bay vs. Cleveland, Nov. 12, 1967
         Indianapolis vs. Denver, Oct. 31, 1988
         Houston vs. Cleveland, Dec. 9, 1990
2nd: 49   Chi. Bears vs. Philadelphia, Nov. 30, 1941
     48   Chi. Cardinals vs. Baltimore, Oct. 2, 1950
         N.Y. Giants vs. Baltimore, Nov. 19, 1950
     45   Cincinnati vs. Houston, Dec. 17, 1972

Most Points, Both Teams, Each Half
1st: 70   Houston (35) vs. Oakland (35), Dec. 22, 1963
     62   N.Y. Jets (41) vs. Tampa Bay (21), Nov. 17, 1985
     59   St. Louis (31) vs. Philadelphia (28), Dec. 16, 1962
2nd: 65   Washington (38) vs. N.Y. Giants (27), Nov. 27, 1966
     62   L.A. Raiders (31) vs. San Diego (31), Jan. 2, 1983
     58   New England (37) vs. Baltimore (21), Nov. 23, 1980
         N.Y. Jets (37) vs. New England (21), Sept. 21, 1987

Most Points, One Quarter
41   Green Bay vs. Detroit, Oct. 7, 1945 (second quarter)
    Los Angeles vs. Detroit, Oct. 29, 1950 (third quarter)
37   Los Angeles vs. Green Bay, Sept. 21, 1980 (second quarter)
35   Chi. Cardinals vs. Boston, Oct. 24, 1948 (third quarter)
    Green Bay vs. Cleveland, Nov. 12, 1967 (first quarter)
    Green Bay vs. Tampa Bay, Oct. 2, 1983 (second quarter)

Most Points, Both Teams, One Quarter
49 Oakland (28) vs. Houston (21), Dec. 22, 1963 (second quarter)
48 Green Bay (41) vs. Detroit (7), Oct. 7, 1945 (second quarter)
   Los Angeles (41) vs. Detroit (7), Oct. 29, 1950 (third quarter)
47 St. Louis (27) vs. Philadelphia (20), Dec. 13, 1964 (second quarter)

Most Points, Each Quarter
1st: 35 Green Bay vs. Cleveland, Nov. 12, 1967
     31 Buffalo vs. Kansas City, Sept. 13, 1964
     28 By seven teams
2nd: 41 Green Bay vs. Detroit, Oct. 7, 1945
     37 Los Angeles vs. Green Bay, Sept. 21, 1980
     35 Green Bay vs. Tampa Bay, Oct. 2, 1983
3rd: 41 Los Angeles vs. Detroit, Oct. 29, 1950
     35 Chi. Cardinals vs. Boston, Oct. 24, 1948
     28 By 10 teams
4th: 31 Oakland vs. Denver, Dec. 17, 1960
        Oakland vs. San Diego, Dec. 8, 1963
        Atlanta vs. Green Bay, Sept. 13, 1981
     28 By many teams

Most Points, Both Teams, Each Quarter
1st: 42 Green Bay (35) vs. Cleveland (7), Nov. 12, 1967
     35 Dall. Texans (21) vs. N.Y. Titans (14), Nov. 11, 1962
        Dallas (28) vs. Philadelphia (7), Oct. 19, 1969
        Kansas City (21) vs. Seattle (14), Dec. 11, 1977
        Detroit (21) vs. L.A. Raiders (14), Dec. 10, 1990
        Dallas (21) vs. Atlanta (14), Dec. 22, 1991
     34 Los Angeles (21) vs. Baltimore (13), Oct. 22, 1950
        Oakland (21) vs. Atlanta (13), Nov. 30, 1975
2nd: 49 Oakland (28) vs. Houston (21), Dec. 22, 1963
     48 Green Bay (41) vs. Detroit (7), Oct. 7, 1945
     47 St. Louis (27) vs. Philadelphia (20), Dec. 13, 1964
3rd: 48 Los Angeles (41) vs. Detroit (7), Oct. 29, 1950
     42 Washington (28) vs. Philadelphia (14), Oct. 1, 1955
     41 Green Bay (21) vs. N.Y. Yanks (20), Oct. 8, 1950
4th: 42 Chi. Cardinals (28) vs. Philadelphia (14), Dec. 7, 1947
        Green Bay (28) vs. Chi. Bears (14), Nov. 6, 1955
        N.Y. Jets (28) vs. Boston (14), Oct. 27, 1968
        Pittsburgh (21) vs. Cleveland (21), Oct. 18, 1969
     41 Baltimore (27) vs. New England (14), Sept. 18, 1978
        New England (27) vs. Baltimore (14), Nov. 23, 1980
     40 Chicago (21) vs. Tampa Bay (19), Nov. 19, 1989

Most Consecutive Games Scoring
322 San Francisco, 1977-97 (current)
274 Cleveland, 1950-71
218 Dallas, 1970-85

Touchdowns

Most Seasons Leading League, Touchdowns
13 Chi. Bears, 1932, 1934-35, 1939, 1941-44, 1946-48, 1956, 1965
 7 Dallas, 1966, 1968, 1971, 1973, 1977-78, 1980
   San Francisco, 1953, 1970, 1987, 1992-95
 6 Oakland, 1967-69, 1972, 1974, 1977
   San Diego, 1963, 1965, 1979, 1981-82, 1985
   Green Bay, 1932, 1937-38, 1961-62, 1996

Most Consecutive Seasons Leading League, Touchdowns
 4 Chi. Bears, 1941-44
   Los Angeles, 1949-52
   San Francisco, 1992-95
 3 Chi. Bears, 1946-48
   Baltimore, 1957-59
   Oakland, 1967-69
 2 By many teams

Most Touchdowns, Season
70 Miami, 1984
66 Houston, 1961
   San Francisco, 1994
64 Los Angeles, 1950

Fewest Touchdowns, Season (Since 1932)
 3 Cincinnati, 1933
 4 Cincinnati/St. Louis, 1934
 5 Detroit, 1942

Most Touchdowns, Game
10 Philadelphia vs. Cincinnati, Nov. 6, 1934
   Los Angeles vs. Baltimore, Oct. 22, 1950
   Washington vs. N.Y. Giants, Nov. 27, 1966
 9 Chi. Cardinals vs. Rochester, Oct. 7, 1923
   Chi. Cardinals vs. N.Y. Giants, Oct. 17, 1948
   Chi. Cardinals vs. N.Y. Bulldogs, Nov. 13, 1949
   Los Angeles vs. Detroit, Oct. 29, 1950
   Pittsburgh vs. N.Y. Giants, Nov. 30, 1952
   Chicago vs. San Francisco, Dec. 12, 1965
   Chicago vs. Green Bay, Dec. 7, 1980
 8 By many teams.

Most Touchdowns, Both Teams, Game
16 Washington (10) vs. N.Y. Giants (6), Nov. 27, 1966
14 Chi. Cardinals (9) vs. N.Y. Giants (5), Oct. 17, 1948

Los Angeles (10) vs. Baltimore (4), Oct. 22, 1950
Houston (7) vs. Oakland (7), Dec. 22, 1963
13 New Orleans (7) vs. St. Louis (6), Nov. 2, 1969
   Kansas City (7) vs. Seattle (6), Nov. 27, 1983 (OT)
   San Diego (8) vs. Pittsburgh (5), Dec. 8, 1985
   N.Y. Jets (7) vs. Miami (6), Sept. 21, 1986 (OT)

Most Consecutive Games Scoring Touchdowns
166 Cleveland, 1957-69
 97 Oakland, 1966-73
 96 Kansas City, 1963-70

Points After Touchdown

Most (One-Point) Points After Touchdown, Season
66 Miami, 1984
65 Houston, 1961
62 Washington, 1983

Fewest (One-Point) Points After Touchdown, Season
 2 Chi. Cardinals, 1933
 3 Cincinnati, 1933
   Pittsburgh, 1934
 4 Cincinnati/St. Louis, 1934

Most (One-Point) Points After Touchdown, Game
10 Los Angeles vs. Baltimore, Oct. 22, 1950
 9 Chi. Cardinals vs. N.Y. Giants, Oct. 17, 1948
   Pittsburgh vs. N.Y. Giants, Nov. 30, 1952
   Washington vs. N.Y. Giants, Nov. 27, 1966
 8 By many teams

Most (One-Point) Points After Touchdown, Both Teams, Game
14 Chi. Cardinals (9) vs. N.Y. Giants (5), Oct. 17, 1948
   Houston (7) vs. Oakland (7), Dec. 22, 1963
   Washington (9) vs. N.Y. Giants (5), Nov. 27, 1966
13 Los Angeles (10) vs. Baltimore (3), Oct. 22, 1950
12 In many games

Most Two-Point Conversions, Season
 6 Miami, 1994
   Minnesota, 1997
 5 Arizona, 1995
   Baltimore, 1996
   Jacksonville, 1996
   Chicago, 1997
 4 By many teams

Most Two-Point Conversions, Game
 3 Baltimore vs. New England, Oct. 6, 1996
 2 Denver vs. Oakland, Oct. 1, 1961
   Oakland vs. San Diego, Sept. 30, 1962
   Kansas City vs. Houston, Oct. 24, 1965
   Houston vs. N.Y. Jets, Dec. 6, 1969
   Seattle vs. Kansas City, Oct. 23, 1994
   Tampa Bay vs. San Francisco, Oct. 23, 1994
   Detroit vs. Green Bay, Nov. 6, 1994
   Washington vs. San Francisco, Nov. 6, 1994
   Carolina vs. New Orleans, Nov. 26, 1995
   Miami vs. Indianapolis, Nov. 26, 1995
   New England vs. Baltimore, Oct. 6, 1996
   Minnesota vs. Seattle, Nov. 10, 1996
   Denver vs. Atlanta, Sept. 28, 1997
   Kansas City vs. St. Louis, Oct. 26, 1997
   Indianapolis vs. Green Bay, Nov. 16, 1997
   Carolina vs. St. Louis, Dec. 20, 1997

Most Two-Point Conversions, Both Teams, Game
 5 Baltimore (3) vs. New England (2), Oct. 6, 1996
 3 Seattle (2) vs. Kansas City (1), Oct. 23, 1994
   Minnesota (2) vs. Seattle (1), Nov. 10, 1996
 2 In many games

Field Goals

Most Seasons Leading League, Field Goals
11 Green Bay, 1935-36, 1940-43, 1946-47, 1955, 1972, 1974
 8 Washington, 1945, 1956, 1971, 1976-77, 1979, 1982, 1992
 7 N.Y. Giants, 1933, 1937, 1939, 1941, 1944, 1959, 1983

Most Consecutive Seasons Leading League, Field Goals
 4 Green Bay, 1940-43
 3 Cleveland, 1952-54
 2 By many teams

Most Field Goals Attempted, Season
49 Los Angeles, 1966
   Washington, 1971
48 Green Bay, 1972
47 N.Y. Jets, 1969
   Los Angeles, 1973
   Washington, 1983

Fewest Field Goals Attempted, Season (Since 1938)
 0 Chi. Bears, 1944
 2 Cleveland, 1939
   Card-Pitt, 1944
   Boston, 1946

OfficeMax®

FREE SOFTWARE!
With Purchase of One of These Quality UMAX® Scanners* ▶

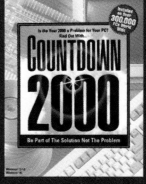

Are you ready for the year 2000? Countdown 2000 software, installed in over 300,000 computers can help you "become part of the solution" by alerting you to year-2000 compatability problems.

THE ASTRA 610P

"The All-in-one Plug'n Play Scanner" – Ideal for home and SOHO. It's parallel interface makes it easy to install. With 300 x 600 dpi hardware resolution enhanced to 4800 x 4800 dpi thru "Ultra View" technology, the 30-bit color scanner offers crystal clear images. It is bundled with Adobe *PhotoDeluxe, Omnipage LE OCR, Presto! PageManager* and *Copy Utility.* 1421-3193

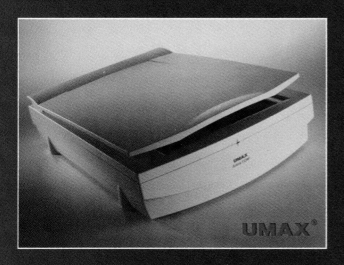

THE ASTRA 1220P

The Astra 1220P captures 36-bit color quality with a resolution of 600 x 1200 dpi (max. 9600 x 9600 dpi), ideal for home or office use. The Astra 1220P easily connects to your PC via parallel/ printer port interface. Scan up to letter size (8.5" x 11.7") documents. Included software: *PhotoDeluxe, PageManager, OmniPage LE OCR* and *Copy Utility.* 1422-3226

Chi. Bears, 1947
3 Chi. Bears, 1945
Cleveland, 1945

Most Field Goals Attempted, Game
9 St. Louis vs. Pittsburgh, Sept. 24, 1967
8 Pittsburgh vs. St. Louis, Dec. 2, 1962
Detroit vs. Minnesota, Nov. 13, 1966
N.Y. Jets vs. Buffalo, Nov. 3, 1968
7 By many teams

Most Field Goals Attempted, Both Teams, Game
11 St. Louis (6) vs. Pittsburgh (5), Nov. 13, 1966
Washington (6) vs. Chicago (5), Nov. 14, 1971
Green Bay (6) vs. Detroit (5), Sept. 29, 1974
Washington (6) vs. N.Y. Giants (5), Nov. 14, 1976
10 In many games

Most Field Goals, Season
37 Carolina, 1996
36 Indianapolis, 1996
35 N.Y. Giants, 1983
L.A. Raiders, 1993

Fewest Field Goals, Season (Since 1932)
0 Boston, 1932, 1935
Chi. Cardinals, 1932, 1945
Green Bay, 1932, 1944
N.Y. Giants, 1932
Brooklyn, 1944
Card-Pitt, 1944
Chi. Bears, 1944, 1947
Boston, 1946
Baltimore, 1950
Dallas, 1952

Most Field Goals, Game
7 St. Louis vs. Pittsburgh, Sept. 24, 1967
Minnesota vs. L.A. Rams, Nov. 5, 1989 (OT)
Dallas vs. Green Bay, Nov. 18, 1996
6 Boston vs. Denver, Oct. 4, 1964
Detroit vs. Minnesota, Nov. 13, 1966
N.Y. Jets vs. Buffalo, Nov. 3, 1968
Philadelphia vs. Houston, Nov. 12, 1972
N.Y. Jets vs. New Orleans, Dec. 3, 1972
St. Louis vs. Atlanta, Dec. 9, 1973
N.Y. Giants vs. Seattle, Oct. 18, 1981
San Francisco vs. New Orleans, Oct. 16, 1983
Pittsburgh vs. Denver, Oct. 23, 1988
San Diego vs. Seattle, Sept. 5, 1993
San Diego vs. Houston, Sept. 19, 1993
Cincinnati vs. Seattle, Nov. 6, 1994
Atlanta vs. New Orleans, Nov. 13, 1994
San Francisco vs. Atlanta, Sept. 29, 1996
Buffalo vs. N.Y. Jets, Oct. 20, 1996
San Diego vs. Oakland, Oct. 5, 1997
5 By many teams

Most Field Goals, Both Teams, Game
9 San Diego (5) vs. Kansas City (4), Sept. 29, 1996
8 Cleveland (4) vs. St. Louis (4), Sept. 20, 1964
Chicago (5) vs. Philadelphia (3), Oct. 20, 1968
Washington (5) vs. Chicago (3), Nov. 14, 1971
Kansas City (5) vs. Buffalo (3), Dec. 19, 1971
Detroit (4) vs. Green Bay (4), Sept. 29, 1974
Cleveland (5) vs. Denver (3), Oct. 19, 1975
New England (4) vs. San Diego (4), Nov. 9, 1975
San Francisco (6) vs. New Orleans (2), Oct. 16, 1983
Seattle (5) vs. L.A. Raiders (3), Dec. 18, 1988
Atlanta (6) vs. New Orleans (2), Nov. 13, 1994
Indianapolis (4) vs. San Diego (4), Nov. 3, 1996
7 In many games

Most Consecutive Games Scoring Field Goals
31 Minnesota, 1968-70
28 Washington, 1988-90
22 San Francisco, 1988-89

Safeties

Most Safeties, Season
4 Cleveland, 1927
Detroit, 1962
Seattle, 1993
San Francisco, 1996
3 By many teams

Most Safeties, Game
3 L.A. Rams vs. N.Y. Giants, Sept. 30, 1984
2 N.Y. Giants vs. Pottsville, Oct. 30, 1927
Chi. Bears vs. Pottsville, Nov. 13, 1927
Detroit vs. Brooklyn, Dec. 1, 1935
N.Y. Giants vs. Pittsburgh, Sept. 17, 1950
N.Y. Giants vs. Washington, Nov. 5, 1961
Chicago vs. Pittsburgh, Nov. 9, 1969

Dallas vs. Philadelphia, Nov. 19, 1972
Los Angeles vs. Green Bay, Oct. 21, 1973
Oakland vs. San Diego, Oct. 26, 1975
Denver vs. Seattle, Jan. 2, 1983
New Orleans vs. Cleveland, Sept. 13, 1987
Buffalo vs. Denver, Nov. 8, 1987
San Francisco vs. St. Louis, Sept. 8, 1996

Most Safeties, Both Teams, Game
3 L.A. Rams (3) vs. N.Y. Giants (0), Sept. 30, 1984
2 Chi. Cardinals (1) vs. Frankford (1), Nov. 19, 1927
Chi. Cardinals (1) vs. Cincinnati (1), Nov. 12, 1933
Chi. Bears (1) vs. San Francisco (1), Oct. 19, 1952
Cincinnati (1) vs. Los Angeles (1), Oct. 22, 1972
Chi. Bears (1) vs. San Francisco (1), Sept. 19, 1976
Baltimore (1) vs. Miami (1), Oct. 29, 1978
Atlanta (1) vs. Detroit (1), Oct. 5, 1980
Houston (1) vs. Philadelphia (1), Oct. 2, 1988
Cleveland (1) vs. Seattle (1), Nov. 14, 1993
Arizona (1) vs. Houston (1), Dec. 4, 1994
(Also see previous record)

First Downs

Most Seasons Leading League
9 Chi. Bears, 1935, 1939, 1941, 1943, 1945, 1947-49, 1955
7 San Diego, 1965, 1969, 1980-83, 1985
6 L.A. Rams, 1946, 1950-51, 1954, 1957, 1973

Most Consecutive Seasons Leading League
4 San Diego, 1980-83
3 Chi. Bears, 1947-49
2 By many teams

Most First Downs, Season
387 Miami, 1984
380 San Diego, 1985
379 San Diego, 1981

Fewest First Downs, Season
51 Cincinnati, 1933
64 Pittsburgh, 1935
67 Philadelphia, 1937

Most First Downs, Game
39 N.Y. Jets vs. Miami, Nov. 27, 1988
Washington vs. Detroit, Nov. 4, 1990 (OT)
38 Los Angeles vs. N.Y. Giants, Nov. 13, 1966
37 Green Bay vs. Philadelphia, Nov. 11, 1962

Fewest First Downs, Game
0 N.Y. Giants vs. Green Bay, Oct. 1, 1933
Pittsburgh vs. Boston, Oct. 29, 1933
Philadelphia vs. Detroit, Sept. 20, 1935
N.Y. Giants vs. Washington, Sept. 27, 1942
Denver vs. Houston, Sept. 3, 1966

Most First Downs, Both Teams, Game
62 San Diego (32) vs. Seattle (30), Sept. 15, 1985
59 Miami (31) vs. Buffalo (28), Oct. 9, 1983 (OT)
Seattle (33) vs. Kansas City (26), Nov. 27, 1983 (OT)
N.Y. Jets (32) vs. Miami (27), Sept. 21, 1986 (OT)
N.Y. Jets (39) vs. Miami (20), Nov. 27, 1988
58 Los Angeles (30) vs. Chi. Bears (28), Oct. 24, 1954
Denver (34) vs. Kansas City (24), Nov. 18, 1974
Atlanta (35) vs. New Orleans (23), Sept. 2, 1979 (OT)
Pittsburgh (36) vs. Cleveland (22), Nov. 25, 1979 (OT)
San Diego (34) vs. Miami (24), Nov. 18, 1984 (OT)
Cincinnati (32) vs. San Diego (26), Sept. 22, 1985

Fewest First Downs, Both Teams, Game
7 Chi. Cardinals (2) vs. Detroit (5), Sept. 15, 1940
9 Pittsburgh (1) vs. Boston (8), Oct. 27, 1935
Boston (4) vs. Brooklyn (5), Nov. 24, 1935
N.Y. Giants (3) vs. Detroit (6), Nov. 7, 1943
Pittsburgh (4) vs. Chi. Cardinals (5), Nov. 11, 1945
N.Y. Bulldogs (1) vs. Philadelphia (8), Sept. 22, 1949
10 N.Y. Giants (4) vs. Washington (6), Dec. 11, 1960

Most First Downs, Rushing, Season
181 New England, 1978
177 Los Angeles, 1973
176 Chicago, 1985

Fewest First Downs, Rushing, Season
36 Cleveland, 1942
Boston, 1944
39 Brooklyn, 1943
40 Philadelphia, 1940
Detroit, 1945

Most First Downs, Rushing, Game
25 Philadelphia vs. Washington, Dec. 2, 1951
23 St. Louis vs. New Orleans, Oct. 5, 1980
21 Cleveland vs. Philadelphia, Dec. 13, 1959
Green Bay vs. Philadelphia, Nov. 11, 1962
Los Angeles vs. New Orleans, Nov. 25, 1973
Pittsburgh vs. Kansas City, Nov. 7, 1976

Continued on page 134

COWBOYS

GREG ELLIS, 6-6, 283, DE, North Carolina, first round (eighth overall) — A blue chip pass rusher who holds the school record with 32.5 career sacks...All America selection as a senior...third player in school history to earn All-Atlantic Coast Conference honors three straight years...finalist for the Lombardi Award... recorded 87 tackles and nine sacks as a senior...had 12.5 sacks as a junior, the second best single-season total in school history behind Lawrence Taylor's UNC record of 16 in 1979...played in four straight bowl games with North Carolina (Sun, Carquest, Gator twice).

FLOZELL ADAMS, 6-7, 335, T, Michigan State, second round (38th overall) — Three-year starter with great size and impressive upper body strength...in 28 career starts, a Spartan back rushed for over 100 yards 17 times...All-America and All-Big Ten selection at tackle as a senior...one of four offensive linemen named as a semi-finalist for the Lombardi Award...Big Ten offensive lineman of the year...blocking led the way as the Spartans averaged 199.5 yards-per-game rushing.

MICHAEL MYERS, 6-2, 286, DL, Alabama, fourth round (100th overall) — Physical run stuffer who can hold his ground...has the ability to play both tackle and end...preseason All-America selection as a senior...earned All-America and All-SEC honors as a junior after transferring from Hinds, Miss., Junior College... led the team with 13 sacks (only Derrick Thomas with 18 in 1987 and 27 in 1988 has posted more sacks for the Tide in a season)...two-time JUCO All-America selection...logged 20 sacks as a freshman.

DARREN HAMBRICK, 6-1, 216, LB, South Carolina, fifth round (130th overall) — Compactly built defender with exceptional quickness (timed at 4.48 in the 40-yard dash)...missed seven games his senior year with a fractured fibula...second-team All-SEC selection as a junior when he recorded 83 tackles...began his college career at the University of Florida...recorded 59 tackles and saw action in every game as a sophomore...made the *Football News* Freshman All-America team in his first year with the Gators.

OLIVER ROSS, 6-4, 300, OL, Iowa State, fifth round (138th overall) — developed into one of the Big 12 Conference's premier drive blockers in just one season at the position...lined up at left tackle and helped the Cyclones average 228.6 yards-per-game passing...helped open holes for the running game to amass 236 yards against Baylor...was an All-Southern California Western State Conference selection as a defensive tackle at Southwestern Community College in Chula Vista, CA...redshirted in 1996 while making the switch from defense to offense.

IZEZLL REESE, 6-2, 193, S, Alabama-Birmingham, sixth round (188th overall) — aggressive pass defender who can unload crunching hits on receivers...All-Conference USA as a strong safety as a senior...made 83 tackles as a senior...finished his career with eight interceptions...had an 85-yard interception return for a touchdown in a 13-7 win over Arkansas State...started every game as a junior and finished second on the team with 69 tackles...started 38-of-44 career games at UAB.

competitive insurance rates for all drivers . . .

Call Progressive and find out how our rate compares with the rates of the competition
— you'll receive a quote on your auto insurance from Progressive Insurance and an "apples-to-apples"
comparison from up to three other leading insurers.

Call 1 800 AUTO PRO®

PROGRESSIVE®

(1-800-288-6776)

or your Authorized Independent Agent.

www.progressive.com

It's a breakthrough any way you look at it.

(actual size)

Introducing the Sony VAIO® 505 SuperSlim notebook computer. • Less than 1 inch thick • Less than 3 pounds • Sleek magnesium-alloy case • Built-in, high-speed modem • i.LINK™ (IEEE-1394) port* • Runs full Windows® 98 • 266 MHz Intel® Pentium® processor w/MMX™ Technology*. Get your VAIO 505 notebook at any local COMP USA or Computer City. For more information on the VAIO 505 notebook see www.sony.com/505

SONY

TARIK SMITH, 5-10, 200, RB, California, seventh round (223rd overall) — Talented athlete who runs with determination and quickness through holes...will break tackles at the line of scrimmage...led team with 162 carries for 636 yards and seven TDs as a senior...averaged 7.1 yards-per-carry as a junior before suffering a season-ending knee injury... had 183 yards in a win over San Jose State and 174 yards and three touchdowns the next week against San Diego State.

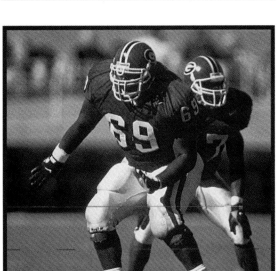

ANTONIO FLEMING, 6-3, 309, G, Georgia, seventh round (227th overall) — Mainstay on the Bulldogs front line...started the last 22 games...helped the Bulldogs to a 10-2 record, including a win over Wisconsin in the Outback Bowl and a No. 10 ranking in the final Associated Press polls as a senior... Georgia averaged 432.6 yards-per-game in 1997 with him at left guard...averaged eight knockdown blocks a game...lined up at right guard as a junior and started every game...saw reserve action at guard as a freshman and sophomore.

RODERICK MONROE, 6-4, 244, TE, Cincinnati, seventh round (237th overall) — Made the transition from basketball to football last season as a senior...became an excellent blocker and possess good speed...started final four games in his first season of football...finished with two receptions for 33 yards and 30 knockdown blocks...also had two receptions in the Bearcats bowl appearance against Utah State...lettered twice on the Bearcats hoop squad (1995-97) as a reserve small forward...transferred to Cincinnati after two years as McLennan, TX, Junior College.

ER
WALKING
/Moisture Guard
$89.95

1998 KIA SPORTAGE
APPROVED FOR CLASS 4 HAZARDOUS TERRAIN
Mountain/High Water/Snow/Dense Forest/Stadium Tailgating
[Available in 8 stylish colors]

EXPLORER

ALPINE CLIMBER
HIGH ALTITUDE/EXTREME CLIMATE BOOT
Extreme Temperature Rating/Reinforced Inner Sole
[Available in sizes 6 - 13]

Starting at
$14,895

XTR³
EXTREME CROSS-TRAINER

It's the ultimate all-terrain outdoor accessory.

With the power to take on a mountain pass

or a highway passing lane with the same cool

confidence. The 1998 Kia Sportage. Engineered

to open up a whole new world of opportunities

with responsive intelligence. Outfitted with

a powerful 16-valve engine, shift-on-the-move

four-wheel drive and a two-speed transfer case.

All supported by a fully boxed ladder frame

and sturdy double-wishbone front suspension.

Test after brutal test, the Sportage stands its own

among harsh environments and critics alike.

And 1998 is no exception. For the second year

in a row, Kia Sportage was proudly named an

IntelliChoice Best Overall Value of the Year.

The 1998 Kia Sportage. The perfect union of

proven SUV engineering and primal instinct.

www.kia.com *1-800-333-4KIA*

S T E T S O N

EASY TO WEAR, HARD TO RESIST.

INDIVIDUAL RECORDS—CAREER

CATEGORY	NAME	PERFORMANCE
Rushing (Yds.)	Tony Dorsett, 1977-87	12,036
Rushing (TDs)	Emmitt Smith, 1990-97	112
Passing (Yds.)	Troy Aikman, 1989-97	26,016
Pass Completions	Troy Aikman, 1989-97	2,292
Passing (TDs.)	Danny White, 1976-88	155
Receiving (No.)	Michael Irvin, 1988-97	666
Receiving (Yds.)	Michael Irvin, 1988-97	10,680
Receiving (TDs)	Bob Hayes, 1965-74	71
Interceptions	Mel Renfro, 1964-77	52
Punting (Avg.)	Mike Saxon, 1985-92	41.4
Punt Return (Avg.)	Bob Hayes, 1965-74	11.1
Kickoff Return (Avg.)	Mel Renfro, 1964-77	26.4
Field Goals (No.)	Rafael Septien, 1978-86	162
Touchdowns (Tot.)	Emmitt Smith, 1990-97	119
Points	Rafael Septien, 1978-86	874

INDIVIDUAL RECORDS—SINGLE SEASON

CATEGORY	NAME	PERFORMANCE
Rushing (Yds.)	Emmitt Smith, 1995	1,773
Rushing (TDs)	Emmitt Smith, 1995	25
Passing (Yds.)	Danny White, 1983	3,980
Pass Completions	Danny White, 1983	334
Passing (TDs)	Danny White, 1983	29
Receiving (No.)	Michael Irvin, 1995	111
Receiving (Yds.)	Michael Irvin, 1995	1,603
Receiving (TDs)	Frank Clarke, 1962	14
Interceptions	Everson Walls, 1981	11
Punting (Avg.)	Sam Baker, 1962	45.4
Punt Return (Avg.)	Bob Hayes, 1968	20.8
Kickoff Return (Avg.)	Mel Renfro, 1965	30.0
Field Goals	Richie Cunningham, 1997	34
Touchdowns (Tot.)	Emmitt Smith, 1995	25
Points	Emmitt Smith, 1995	150

INDIVIDUAL RECORDS—SINGLE GAME

CATEGORY	NAME	PERFORMANCE
Rushing (Yds.)	Emmitt Smith, 10/31/93 (@Phil)	237
Rushing (TDs)	Calvin Hill, 9/19/71 (@Buf)	4
	Emmitt Smith, 12/16/90 (Phoe)	
	Emmitt Smith, 9/4/95 (@ NYG)	
Passing (Yds.)	Don Meredith, 11/10/63 (@SF)	460
Passing (TDs)	Seven times, last by	5
	Danny White, 10/20/83 (@NYG)	
Receiving (No.)	Lance Rentzel, 11/19/67 (Wash)	13
Receiving (Yds.)	Bob Hayes, 11/13/66 (@Wash)	246
Receiving (TDs)	Bob Hayes, 12/20/70 (Hou)	4
Interceptions	Herb Adderley, 9/26/71 (@Phil)	3
	Lee Roy Jordan, 11/4/73 (Cin)	
	Dennis Thurman, 12/13/81 (Phil)	
Field Goals	Chris Boniol, 11/18/96 (Green Bay)	7
Touchdowns (Tot.)	Six times, last by	4
	Emmitt Smith 9/4/95 (@NYG)	
Points	Six times, last by	24
	Emmitt Smith, 9/4/95 (@NYG)	

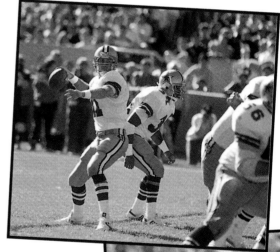

Seven members of the Pro Football Hall of Fame in Canton, Ohio, have been elected based on their accomplishments with the Cowboys— Bob Lilly in 1980, Roger Staubach in 1985, Tom Landry in 1990, Tex Schramm in 1991, Tony Dorsett and Randy White in 1994 and Mel Renfro in 1996.

TEX SCHRAMM

Tex Schramm helped build the Cowboys into "America's Team" as President and General Manager from 1960 to 1989. As Director of day-to-day operations for the Cowboys, Schramm kept Dallas on the cutting edge of technology and promotions throughout his career. Schramm played a prominent role in the AFL-NFL merger and served as chairman of the NFL's Competition Committee from 1966-88.

BOB LILLY

Lilly, the first college player ever drafted by the Cowboys, was selected to play in the Pro Bowl 11 times while playing for Dallas from 1961 to 1974. Lilly came to the Cowboys after a collegiate career at Texas Christian University.

TOM LANDRY

Tom Landry compiled an overall record of 270-178-6 with two World Championships as the head coach of the Cowboys from 1960 to 1989. A native of Mission, Tex., Landry helped build the Cowboys from the ground up and was responsible for the development of the flex defense and the shotgun offense.

1999 SWIMSUIT CALENDAR

DALLAS COWBOYS
Cheerleaders
AMERICA'S SWEETHEARTS

JANUARY

ROGER STAUBACH

Staubach, known as "Captain Comeback" to Dallas fans, quarterbacked the Cowboys to four NFC Championships and victories in Super Bowl VI and XII. Staubach, a native of Cincinnati and a graduate of the U.S. Naval Academy, played for Dallas from 1969 to 1979.

RANDY WHITE

White, a nine-time Pro Bowler during his 14 year career with Dallas, was co-MVP of Super Bowl XII in the Cowboys 27-10 win over Denver. White joined the Cowboys as a first-round draft choice in 1975 and played for Dallas from 1975 to 1988.

TONY DORSETT

Dorsett, the Cowboys all-time leading rusher, stands fourth all-time on the NFL's career rushing list with 12,739 yards. Dorsett, the 1976 Heisman Trophy winner from the University of Pittsburgh, played with Dallas from 1977 to 1987.

MEL RENFRO

Renfro, a Pro Bowler in each of his first 10 seasons in the NFL, is the club's all-time interception leader with 52. He also holds the club record for career kickoff return average at 26.4 yards. Renfro joined the Cowboys as a second-round draft choice in 1964 and played for Dallas until 1977.

Tex Schramm, Bedford Wynne, Clint Murchison and Tom Landry in front of the team's original offices in 1960.

1960

LANDRY HIRED - Clint Murchison, Jr., and Bedford Wynne sign N.Y. Giants defensive assistant Tom Landry to a personal services contract on Dec. 27, 1959, with the intention of naming him head coach once they are awarded an expansion franchise by the NFL.

NFL FRANCHISE - Clint Murchison, Jr. and Bedford Wynne were awarded an expansion franchise in the NFL at the annual league meeting in Miami Beach, Fla. The Cowboys were to play as a swing team, playing every other team one time during the first season, although listed in the Western Conference standings (January 28).

COWBOYS STOCKED - A player pool was set up in the league meeting in Los Angeles, with each of 12 NFL teams freezing 25 names on its roster and the Cowboys allowed to pick three from each team for a total of 36 veterans. Dallas, once given the list, had to select its 36 players within 24 hours (March 13).

TRAINING STARTS - Rookies report to first Cowboys camp at Pacific University in Forest Grove, Oregon (July 9).
FIRST PRE-SEASON GAME - The Cowboys, less than six months in existence, get their first test and drop a 16-10 preseason game to San Francisco in Seattle (August 6).

FIRST HOME GAME - In their Dallas debut, in the Salesmanship Club preseason game, the Cowboys led the world champion Baltimore Colts into the final minute before a 62-yard pass from Johnny Unitas to Lenny Moore gave the Colts a 14-10 victory (August 19).

FIRST VICTORY —In a preseason game at Louisville, KY, the Cowboys beat New York's Giants, 14-3, with Frank Clarke catching touchdown passes for 73 yards (Eddie LeBaron) and 74 yards (Don Meredith) (August 27).

FIRST LEAGUE GAME - In their first league game, Dallas fell to Pittsburgh, 35-28, with Bobby Layne leading a fourth-period Steelers rally (Sept. 24, Saturday night).

STREAK SNAPPED - Dallas snaps a 10-game losing streak by tying New York, 31-31, at Yankee Stadium (Dec. 4).

1961

TRAINING STARTS - Rookies launch training at new campsite - St. Olaf College in Northfield, Minn. (July 9).
FIRST LEAGUE WIN - Scoring ten points in the final 56 seconds, the Cowboys score their first NFL victory, 27-24, over Pittsburgh in the '61 league opener in the Cotton Bowl. Allen Green's 27-yard field goal on the game's final play won it before 23,500 (Sept. 17).

1962

TRAINING STARTS - Team begins training at new campsite - Northern Michigan College in Marquette, Mich. (July 13).

PENALTY HISTORY - For the first time in anyone's memory in a NFL game, points were awarded for a penalty. The Cowboys were detected holding in the end zone on a 99-yd. TD pass from LeBaron

Coach Tom Landry opens the Cowboys first training camp at Pacific University in Forest Grove, OR.

FESTINA™

FESTINA. IT'S ABOUT TIME.™

FESTINA, the fastest growing watch line in Europe, has finally arrived in North America. Pictured above Richard Virenque, world class rider for the Festina Racing Team and the new Mecaquartz.™ As the Official Timer of the Tour de France, we understand the importance of a split-second. **FESTINA. It's About Time.™**

Beasley's Jewelry
177 W. Main Street, Lewisville
214-221-4641

Don Meredith quarterbackbacked the Cowboys from1960-68.

to Clarke, and Pittsburgh was awarded a safety. The Steelers eventually won 30-28 (Sept. 23).

100-YARD FIRSTS - Cowboys' Amos Marsh returned a kickoff 101 yards and Mike Gaechter returned a pass interception 100 yards, both plays for fourth-quarter TDs in a 41-19 win over Philadelphia in Dallas. It was the first time in NFL history that two 100-yard runs had been made in the same game, much less by the same team in the same quarter (Oct. 14).

1963

SHIFT TO KANSAS CITY - The rival Dallas Texans of the AFL announce they are moving the franchise to Kansas City (Feb. 8).

CALIFORNIA TRAINING SITE - The Cowboys open training at California Lutheran College in Thousand Oaks, Calif. (July 12).

HOWTON SETS RECORD - Bill Howton broke Don Hutson's all-time receiving mark with a 14-yard catch against Washington (there). Hutson's record was 7,991 yards and the catch gave Howton an even 8,000 yards (Sept. 29).

1964

LANDRY CONTRACT - With one year to go on his original contract, Tom Landry is signed to a 10-year extension, in effect giving him an 11-year pact, possibly the longest in major pro sports history (Feb. 5).

1965

FIRST SELLOUT - An overflow crowd of 76,251 jams the Cotton Bowl for the Cleveland game, notching the team's first home sellout. Cleveland won, 24-17 (Nov. 21).

1966

PLAYOFF BOWL - After defeating New York, 38-20, in the season finale (and winning five of their last seven games) to get into the Playoff Bowl at Miami, the Cowboys fall to Baltimore, 35-3 (Jan. 15).

MERGER - Peace comes to pro football with Cowboys General Manager Tex Schramm completing two months of negotiations with AFL's Lamar Hunt, merging the two leagues under the NFL banner (June 8).

SCHRAMM ELEVATED - Texas E. Schramm, Vice-President and General Manager of the Cowboys from the beginning, was named President of the club by Owner Clint Murchison, Jr., who retained the title of Chairman of the Board.

NEELY CASE SOLVED - Dallas and Houston reached agreement in the Ralph Neely case. Neely remained with Dallas, with Houston receiving the Cowboys Nos. 1, 2 and two fifth round picks in the 1967 draft (Nov. 17).

THE CHAMPIONSHIP - The Cowboys won their first championship, capturing the Eastern Conference title with a 10-3-1 record, but lost the NFL Championship Game to Green Bay, 34-27.

LEROY NEIMAN

Leroy Neiman '93

38"x29"

PUT A WILD SPIN ON YOUR ORLANDO VACATION!

TWISTER
RIDE IT OUT ℠

Step into one of the most action-packed movies of all time: TWISTER! Grab onto the railing and "Ride It Out," as the swirling vortex of a tornado blows you away!

TO BOOK UNIVERSAL STUDIOS® VACATION PACKAGES, CALL 1-800-589-9911

UNIVERSAL STUDIOS FLORIDA®

1967

TEXAS STADIUM - On Dec. 23, Owner Clint Murchison, Jr., formally announced plans to build Texas Stadium in suburban Irving. The stadium, to be financed through a bond-option plan, would be ready for the 1970 season. The stadium would seat a minimum of 58,000.

SECOND CHAMPIONSHIP - Under the NFL's new format, the Cowboys easily won the Capitol Division and defeated Cleveland, Century Division winner, 52-14, in the Cotton Bowl for the Eastern conference championship. However, on Dec. 31 in Green Bay, the Cowboys lost their second bid for an NFL title, falling to the Packers, 21-17, in the 13 degree below weather.

1968

WIN CAPITOL - For the second straight year the Cowboys won the Capitol Division, but for the first time in three years the Cowboys did not win the Eastern Championship, being upset at Cleveland, 31-20, on Dec. 21. Dallas won the Runner-Up Bowl over Minnesota, 17-13.

1969

TEXAS STADIUM - Ground was broken for Texas Stadium in suburban Irving on January 25, and on June 29, Bert Rose was named general manager of the stadium.

ORIGINALS RETIRE - An era ended for the Cowboys in July. On July 5th at a press conference in Dallas, quarterback Don Meredith, the last of the original Cowboys, announced his retirement. Then, on July 18th, the day the veterans were to report to training camp, all-time rushing great Don Perkins officially retired.

REPEAT CAPITOL WINS - Once again the Cowboys rolled to the Capitol Division Championship with an 11-2-1 season. However, the Cowboys failed to win the Eastern Championship when on Dec. 28, the Cowboys lost to Cleveland, 38-14, in the Cotton Bowl.

1970

FIVE STRAIGHT PLAYOFFS - The Cowboys won their last five games to finish 10-4, claim the Eastern Division championship and make the playoffs for the fifth year in a row. They defeated Detroit, 5-0, in the opening round to get a shot at the National Conference championship.

FIRST NFC TITLE - The Cowboys captured the biggest prize of their 11-year history on Jan. 3 when they downed San Francisco, 17-10, for the NFC crown. A 16-13 loss to Baltimore in the Super Bowl Jan. 17 left Dallas with one major goal still unrealized.

1971

TEXAS STADIUM - The Cowboys opened a new era in their sparkling Irving, Tex., home with a 44-21 victory over the New England Patriots on Oct. 24. Duane Thomas scored the first touchdown in the new stadium, a 56-yard run just two minutes and 16 seconds after the opening kickoff. Attendance was 65,708.

SIX STRAIGHT PLAYOFFS - The Cowboys won their last seven games to finish 11-3, claim the Eastern Division championship and make the playoffs for the sixth year in a row. They defeated Minnesota, 20-12, in the opening round.

SECOND NFC TITLE - For the second consecutive year, the Cowboys met the San Francisco 49ers in the National Conference showdown. This time Dallas won 14-13 to qualify for its second straight Super Bowl.

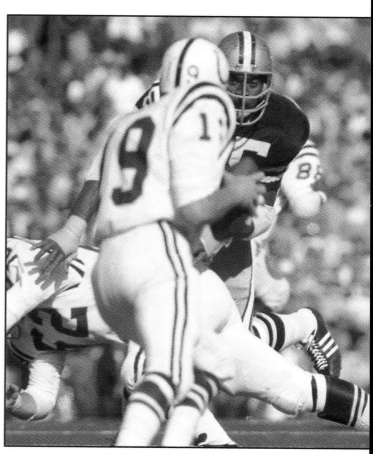

Jethro Pugh led the Cowboys in sacks for five straight years between 1968-72.

Tom Landry is carried off the field following the Cowboys 24-3 win over Miami in Super Bowl VI.

FIRST WORLD CHAMPIONSHIP - The Cowboys downed the Miami Dolphins, 24-3, to win Super Bowl VI in New Orleans on Jan. 16. It was the 10th victory in a row for Dallas as Roger Staubach passed for two touchdowns and was named the game's Most Valuable Player.

1972

FIRST 1,000-YARD BACK - Calvin Hill became the first Dallas player to rush for 1,000 yards when he gained 111 on Dec. 9 against the Washington Redskins in Texas Stadium. Hill wound up with 1,036 yards for the season on a record 245 carries.

SEVEN STRAIGHT PLAYOFFS - The Cowboys qualified for the NFL playoffs a record seventh consecutive year, their 10-4 record earning them the National Conference Wild Card berth. Roger Staubach passed for two touchdowns in the last 1:30 to give the Cowboys a 30-28 victory at San Francisco in the first round. Then, at Washington on New Year's Eve, Dallas was foiled in its bid for a third straight NFL title with the Redskins win, 16-3.

1973

100 VICTORIES - The Cowboys and Coach Tom Landry recorded their 100th victory with a 40-3 Texas Stadium win over the New Orleans Saints on Sept. 24. Landry ended the season with a career mark of 108-80-6 to rank ninth on the list of the NFL's all-time winningest coaches.

EIGHT STRAIGHT PLAYOFFS - The Cowboys regained the NFC Eastern Division title with a 10-4 record and broke their own NFL record by reaching the playoffs for the eighth year in a row. Dallas defeated the Western Division champion Los Angeles Rams in the first round, 27-16, but fell to Central Division winner Minnesota in the NFC Championship Game, 27-10.

1974

FIRST TOP DRAFT CHOICE - For the first time in their history, the Cowboys had the very first choice in the NFL Draft. The No. 1 pick came to Dallas from Houston in exchange for Tody Smith and Billy Parks. The Cowboys selected Ed "Too Tall" Jones, a 6-9, 260-pound defensive end from Tennessee State.

PLAYOFFS MISSED - The Cowboys' record breaking string of eight straight years in the NFL playoffs was broken when the club's 8-6 record failed to qualify.

1975

LILLY HONORED - "Mr. Cowboy" was honored on Bob Lilly Day at Texas Stadium at halftime of the Philadelphia game on Nov. 23. It was first such recognition ever given to a Dallas player. Lilly never missed a game in 14 years with the Cowboys, earning All-Pro honors seven times at defensive tackle before retiring prior to the '75 season.

TEN STRAIGHT WINNING SEASONS - The Cowboys' 10-4 record earned them the NFC Wild Card berth in the playoffs. The composite record over 10 straight winning seasons was 101-37-2.

THIRD NFC TITLE - After shocking Minnesota in the first round, 17-14, on Roger Staubach's 50-yard "Hail Mary" pass to Drew Pearson,

COINCIDENCE?

If NFL™ football and Miller Lite weren't made for each other, how do you explain the <u>uncanny</u> resemblance between these two objects?

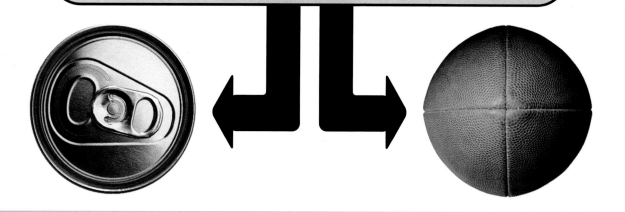

The letter "L" appears twice in both the words *football* and *Miller*.... Think about it.

Plus, a football helmet sort of has the same shape as the top of a Miller Lite can. **What are the odds of that?** Whatever, it's still a good bet that you all will want to enjoy a Miller Lite beer just thinking about it.

Another strange coincidence? There are 100 yards in a football field. A six-pack of Miller Lite contains 72 ounces of beer. A difference of only 28. Scary, huh?

www.millerlite.com

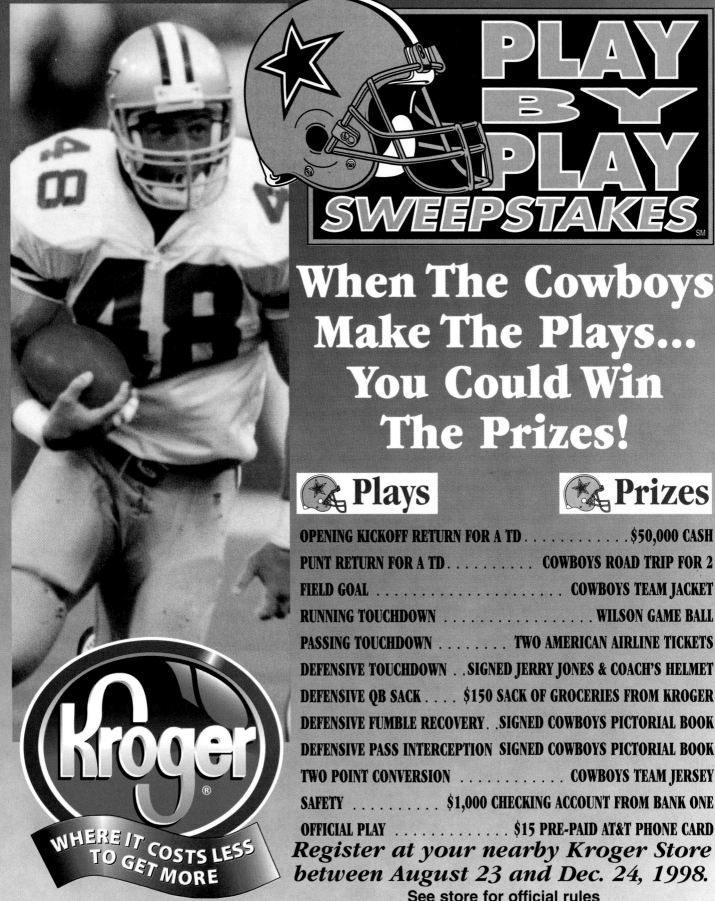

the Cowboys traveled to Los Angeles for the NFC showdown. Staubach threw four touchdown passes, three to Preston Pearson, and Dallas won, 37-7. Pittsburgh won Super Bowl X on Jan. 18 in Miami, 21-17.

1976

MEREDITH, PERKINS HONORED - Former Cowboys greats Don Meredith and Don Perkins joined Bob Lilly in the Ring of Honor at Texas Stadium during halftime ceremonies at the New York Giants game on Nov. 7.

ELEVEN STRAIGHT WINNING SEASONS - The Cowboys won the NFC Eastern Division title with their 11-3 record, giving them their 11th straight winning season and 10th playoff berth in that period. A 14-12 first round loss to Los Angeles - the first time Dallas had lost in the first round under the current playoff setup - ended the season.

1977

HOWLEY HONORED - Former All-Pro linebacker Chuck Howley, a Cowboy from 1961 through 1973, became the fourth member of the Ring of Honor. Howley was honored during ceremonies at halftime of the Detroit Lions game on Oct. 30.

TWELVE STRAIGHT WINNING SEASONS - Getting off to an 8-0 start, their best ever, the Cowboys rolled to a 12-2 record, the championship of the NFC East, and their 12th consecutive winning season. They opened their 11th visit to the playoffs in those 12 years with a 37-7 first-round victory over the Chicago Bears at Texas Stadium.

FOURTH NFC TITLE - Dallas crushed the Minnesota Vikings at Texas Stadium, 23-6, for National Conference crown No. 4 and the right to meet the Denver Broncos in Super Bowl XII.

SECOND WORLD CHAMPIONSHIP - The Cowboys stopped the Denver Broncos, 27-10, to win Super Bowl XII in New Orleans on January 15, 1978. In the process, Dallas tied Minnesota for most Super Bowl appearances (four) and Green Bay, Miami and Pittsburgh for most Super Bowl victores (two). Defensive linemen Harvey Martin and Randy White were named co-Most Valuable Players in the game.

1978

THIRTEEN STRAIGHT WINNING SEASONS - After a mediocre 6-4 start, the Cowboys won six straight games to finish the expanded regular season with a 12-4 record and their 10th division crown. It marked the Cowboys' 13th consecutive winning season and 12th trip to the playoffs in that span. Dallas rallied to beat Atlanta 27-20

in a divisional playoff at Texas Stadium, sending the Cowboys to their seventh NFC championship game in the past nine years.

FIFTH NFC TITLE - Dallas shut out the Rams in Los Angeles 28-0 in the National Conference title game to advance to the Super Bowl a record fifth time, including three of the last four. In the first Super Bowl rematch, Pittsburgh edged the Cowboys 35-31 for the NFL championship on Jan. 21 in Miami's Orange Bowl.

1979

TWENTIETH ANNIVERSARY - The Cowboys celebrated their 20th anniversary season at halftime of the St. Louis Cardinals game at Texas Stadium on Oct. 21. Stars from each of those 20 seasons plus Coach Tom Landry were introduced during the halftime ceremonies.

FOURTH STRAIGHT NFC EAST TITLE - Rallying from a mid-season slump, the Cowboys won their final three games to finish with an 11-5 record, their 11th division championship, including the past four NFC East titles, and 14th consecutive winning season. The Cowboys made their 13th trip to the playoffs in those 14 years, but were eliminated by Los Angeles 21-19 in a divisional playoff at Texas Stadium.

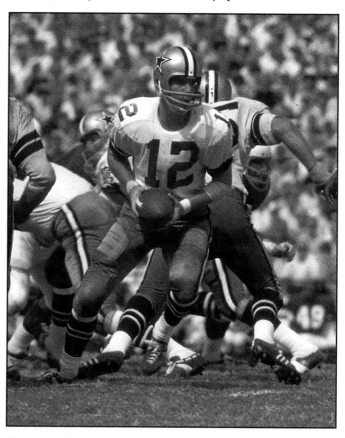

Roger Staubach retires in early 1980 after 11 record breaking years with the Cowboys.

1980

STAUBACH RETIRES - At a press conference at Texas Stadium on March 31, quarterback Roger Staubach announced his retirement after 11 record-breaking years with the Cowboys. Staubach held all major Cowboys' passing records and was the all-time leading NFL passer.

LILLY ENTERS HALL OF FAME - Bob Lilly, a seven-time All-Pro defensive tackle in his 14-year career with the Cowboys from 1961-74, became the first Cowboys' player to be inducted into the Pro Football Hall of Fame. Enshrined along with Lilly on Aug. 2 at Canton, Ohio, were Herb Adderley, who played for the Cowboys from 1970-71, Jim Otto and Deacon Jones.

FIFTEEN STRAIGHT WINNING SEASONS - Behind new starting quarterback Danny White, the Cowboys rolled to their 15th consecutive winning season with a surprising 12-4 record, tied for best in the league with Philadelphia and Atlanta. The Cowboys lost the NFC East title to Philadelphia on a tie-breaker, but entered the playoffs for the 14th time in 15 years, this time as a wild card team. The Cowboys beat Los Angeles 34-13 at Texas Stadium in the NFC Wild Card Game and rallied past the Falcons at Atlanta 30-27 to advance to the NFC Championship Game at Philadelphia. But the Cowboys lost 20-7 in their bid for a sixth Super Bowl appearance.

LANDRY'S 200th VICTORY - Tom Landry joined George Halas and Curly Lambeau as the only coaches with 200 NFL victories when the Cowboys beat Los Angeles 34-13 on Dec. 28 at Texas Stadium in the NFC Wild Card Game, raising Landry's record to 200-119-6, counting regular season and playoff games.

1981

RENFRO HONORED - Former All-Pro defensive back Mel Renfro, the Cowboys' all-time leading pass interceptor, became the fifth member of the Cowboys' Ring of Honor. Renfro, who played for Dallas from 1964 through 1977, was honored during halftime ceremonies of the Cowboys-Miami Dolphins game at Texas Stadium Oct. 25.

TWELFTH DIVISION CHAMPIONSHIP - The Cowboys regained the NFC Eastern Division Championship, their 12th division title since 1966, with a 12-4 record and tied Oakland's NFL mark of 16 consecutive winning seasons. Entering the playoffs for the 15th time in that span, the Cowboys advanced to the NFC Championship Game for the ninth time in 12 years by routing Tampa Bay 38-0 at Texas Stadium. But for the second year in a row, Dallas lost the conference title game. San Francisco scored a last-minute touchdown at Candlestick Park to edge the Cowboys 28-27 for a berth in Super Bowl XVI.

1982

200TH REGULAR-SEASON VICTORY - The Cowboys beat Washington 24-10 at RFK Stadium on Dec. 5 for the club's and Coach Tom Landry's 200th regular season victory.

SEVENTEEN STRAIGHT WINNING SEASONS - The Cowboys finished the strike-shortened regular season with a 6-3 record to establish an NFL record of 17 consecutive winning seasons. Entering the playoffs for a record-tying eighth straight year and for the 16th time in 17 years, the Cowboys beat Tampa Bay 30-17 and Green Bay 37-26, both at Texas Stadium, to advance to the NFC Championship Game for the third year in a row. But again the Cowboys come up short, losing 31-17 at Washington.

1983

STAUBACH HONORED - Former quarterback Roger Staubach, who led the Cowboys to four Super Bowls, became the sixth member of the Ring of Honor during halftime ceremonies of the Cowboys-Tampa Bay game on Oct. 9.

NEW HEADQUARTERS - Ground was broken on Nov. 29 for the Cowboys' new headquarters and training facility in Valley Ranch in northwest Dallas County.

EIGHTEEN STRAIGHT WINNING SEASONS - The Cowboys extended their NFL record to 18 consecutive winning seasons with a 12-4 finish. The club also set a league record with its ninth straight playoff appearance, qualifying as a wild card entry. The Los Angeles Rams eliminated the Cowboys from the playoffs, however, with a 24-17 upset victory at Texas Stadium in the NFC Wild Card Game on Dec. 26.

1984

SILVER SEASON - The Cowboys kicked off their 25th anniversary with a news conference at Texas Stadium on Jan. 27. President Tex Schramm announced the Cowboys would celebrate their 25th anniversary during 1984 under the theme "Silver Season."

OWNERSHIP CHANGES HANDS - The sale of the Cowboys from the Murchison family to an 11-member limited partnership headed by Dallas businessman H.R. "Bum" Bright was approved by NFL owners on March 19 at the league's annual meeting in Honolulu. The sale was completed on May 18.

NINETEEN STRAIGHT WINNING SEASONS - The Cowboys defeated the Eagles 26-10 in Philadelphia to extend their NFL record to 19

GO LONG.

Combine great football with a great vacation. The 1999 Pro Bowl will kick off in Hawaii's Aloha Stadium, February 7, on the Island of O'ahu. And there are five more Islands of Aloha you can touch down in before or after the game. Each island is unique. Each one is filled with an abundance of things to see and do. And everywhere you go, you'll be welcomed with warm smiles and the Aloha Spirit.

The top players in the NFL have to go through a whole season of hard knocks to get here. All you have to do is pick up the phone and call your travel agent.

HAWAI'I®
The Islands of Aloha

1-800-GOHAWAII   www.gohawaii.com

HOME TEAM FAVORITE WITH THE
DALLAS COWBOYS

DR PEPPER BOTTLING
COMPANY OF TEXAS

consecutive winning seasons. The Cowboys finished 9-7 and missed the playoffs for the first time in 10 years and only the second time in 19 years.

1985

STAUBACH ENTERS HALL OF FAME - Roger Staubach, the master of the comeback victory during his 11-year career as a Cowboys quarterback, was inducted into the Pro Football Hall of Fame in his first year of eligibility. Enshrined with Staubach on Aug. 3 at Canton, Ohio, were Pete Rozelle, Joe Namath, O.J. Simpson and Frank Gatski. Staubach joined Bob Lilly as the only players who spent their entire career with the Cowboys to be elected to the Hall of Fame.

TEXAS STADIUM IMPROVEMENTS - Texas Stadium unveiled a new look when the Cowboys opened their preseason schedule against Green Bay on Aug. 10. The stadium became the first to have two

Tony Dorsett ran for 12,739 yards in his NFL career, including a league record 99 yard touchdown run at Minnesota in 1983.

DiamondVision color scoreboards, and the addition of 118 Crown Suites gave Texas Stadium more private suites, 296, than any stadium in the nation.

COWBOYS RANCH OPENS - Cowboys players and coaches reported on Aug. 27 to the team's new headquarters and training facility at Cowboys Center in Valley Ranch.

DORSETT PASSES 10,000 YARDS - On a 19-yard sweep around left end, Tony Dorsett, became the sixth player in NFL history to rush for 10,000 yards. Dorsett's feat highlighted a 27-13 victory over Pittsburgh at Texas Stadium on Oct. 13.

THIRTEENTH DIVISION CHAMPIONSHIP - The Cowboys edged the New York Giants 28-21 on Dec. 15 at Texas Stadium to capture the NFC Eastern Division championship for the first time since 1981. Picked in most season previews to finish third or fourth in the division, the Cowboys rallied for their NFL record 20th consecutive winning season, a 13th division title in 20 years and a playoff berth for the 18th time in that span. But in their NFL record 36th playoff game appearance, the Cowboys fell 20-0 to the Los Angeles Rams in Anaheim on Jan. 4.

1986

COWBOYS GO TO LONDON - The Cowboys began preparations for their first trip to a foreign country when the NFL announced on March 12 that the Cowboys would play the Super Bowl champion Chicago Bears in a preseason game at London's Wembley Stadium on Aug. 3.

100TH WIN AT TEXAS STADIUM - Dallas defeated St. Louis 37-6 for the club's 100th victory at Texas Stadium. Since the facility opened in 1971 the Cowboys have compiled a 100-25 (.800) record. STREAK BROKEN - The Cowboys' streak of 20 consecutive winning seasons from 1966 through 1985, third longest in professional sports history, came to an end when the club finished with a 7-9 record after losing seven of its last eight games. Only baseball's New York Yankees (39 straight winning seasons, 1962-64) and hockey's Montreal Canadiens (32 from 1951-52 through 1982-83) surpassed the Cowboys' accomplishments. After the 1986 season, the Washington Redskins' five straight winning campaigns (1982-86) represented the NFL's longest active streak.

1987

FOUNDER DIES - Cowboys founder Clint Murchison, Jr., died March 30 after a long illness. Murchison, 63, who owned the club until

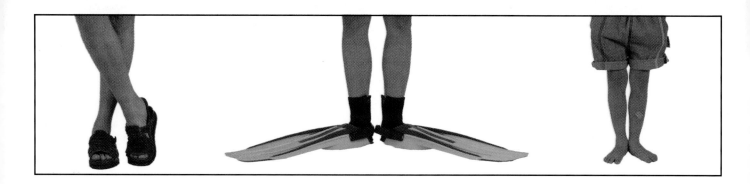

HEALTHCARE FOR

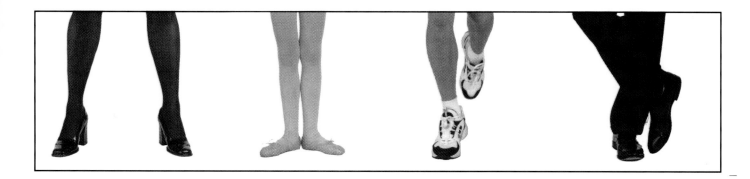

ALL WALKS OF LIFE.

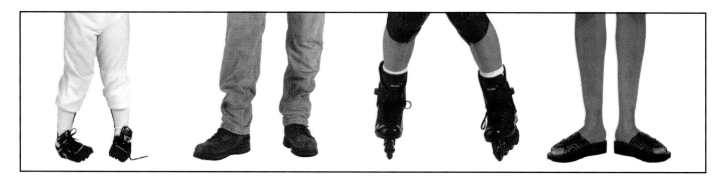

QualityCare*Network*.

Denton Regional Medical Center • Las Colinas Medical Center • Medical Center Dallas-Southwest • Medical Center of Arlington
Medical Center of Lancaster • Medical Center of Lewisville • Medical Center of McKinney • Medical Center of Plano
Medical City Dallas • Medical City Dallas Children's Hospital • North Hills Hospital • Plaza Medical Center of Fort Worth

Official healthcare provider for the Dallas Cowboys, Texas Rangers and Texas Motor Speedway.
For more information or free physician referral call 1-800-265-8624.

1984, acquired the expansion Dallas franchise in the NFL in 1960. He hired Tex Schramm as general manager, gave Tom Landry a 10-year contract when his coaching career was in doubt in 1964 and was instrumental in the building of Texas Stadium.

DORSETT GETS 12,000 YARDS - Tony Dorsett became the fourth rusher in NFL history to gain more than 12,000 yards when he registered 52 yards against the Rams on Dec. 21 for a career total of 12,036. The only runners ahead of Dorsett were Walter Payton, Jim Brown and Franco Harris.

1988

LANDRY TIES LAMBEAU - Dallas opened the 1988 season against Pittsburgh on Sept. 12 and Tom Landry tied a NFL record held by Curly Lambeau by coaching in his 29th consecutive season with the same team. Lambeau led the Green Bay Packers from 1921-49.

1989

JONES ACQUIRES COWBOYS, NAMED JOHNSON COACH - Jerry Jones reached an agreement to purchase the Cowboys from Bum Bright on Feb. 25 and announced that University of Miami Coach Jimmy Johnson would replace Tom Landry.

SALE APPROVED, SCHRAMM RESIGNS - The sale of the Cowboys to Jerry Jones was unanimously approved by NFL owners on April 18 at a special meeting in New York. At the same meeting, Tex Schramm was named president of the new World League of American Football. He announced his resignation as president and general manager of the Cowboys after 29 years with the club.

AIKMAN SIGNED - The Cowboys, holding the No. 1 pick in the NFL Draft for only the second time in their history, announced the signing of quarterback Troy Aikman to a six-year contract on April 20.

JORDAN HONORED - Former All-Pro linebacker Lee Roy Jordan, a Cowboy from 1963-76, became the seventh member of the Ring of Honor. Jordan was honored during ceremonies at halftime of the Phoenix Cardinals game on Oct. 29.

1990

AUSTIN TRAINING CAMP - Beginning on July 18, nearly 100,000 fans visit the Cowboys' first ever in-state training camp at St. Edward's University in Austin.

LANDRY ENTERS HALL OF FAME - Tom Landry, who led the Cowboys to five Super Bowls and 20 consecutive winning seasons as the Cowboys head coach from 1960-88, was inducted into the Pro Football Hall of Fame in his first year of eligibility. Enshrined on Aug. 4 at Canton, Ohio, Landry joined former Dallas players Bob Lilly and Roger Staubach as the only Hall of Fame members who built their achievements with the Cowboys.

SMITH ROOKIE OF THE YEAR, JOHNSON COACH OF THE YEAR - Following a dramatic turn-around season where the team posted a 7-9 record and missed the playoffs by one game, Jimmy Johnson was named the NFL Coach of the Year by the Associated Press. Running back Emmitt Smith, who led all NFL rookie running backs in rushing yardage and touchdowns, was named the A.P.'s NFC Offensive Rookie of the Year.

1991

RECORD DRAFT HAUL INCLUDES MARYLAND AS NO. 1 OVERALL PICK - After a pre-draft trade with the New England Patriots, the Cowboys used the No. 1 overall selection in the NFL Draft for only the third time in franchise history. Dallas chose Outland Trophy winner Russell Maryland (DT) with the top pick. The Cowboys went on to acquire 16 more choices, setting a club record for most selections in a 12-round draft with 17 overall.

SCHRAMM ENTERS HALL OF FAME —One of the NFL's true innovators, and the guiding force behind the development of America's Team, Tex Schramm was inducted into the Pro Football Hall of Fame on July 27, 1991. Schramm, who served as the President and General Manager of the Dallas Cowboys from the team's conception in 1960 until his retirement in 1989, joined Staubach, Lilly and Landry with his enshrinement in Canton, Ohio.

RETURN TO THE PLAYOFFS - After winning the final five games of the season, Dallas finished with an 11-5 record - the team's best mark since the 1983 season. The initial spark to the winning streak was a 24-21 win over the eventual World Champion Washington Redskins on Nov. 24. The win, at Washington's RFK Stadium, ended the Redskins' bid for a perfect regular season after 11 straight wins. Dallas finished second in the NFC East and qualified as the NFC's No. 2 Wild Card Playoff entry, marking the club's first postseason trip since 1985. Dallas traveled to Chicago and defeated the Bears 17-13 in the opening round Wild Card Game before dropping a 38-6 decision at Detroit the following week.

SMITH AND IRVIN LEAD NFL - Running back Emmitt Smith and wide receiver Michael Irvin became the first two players from the same team to lead the NFL in rushing yardage and receiving yardage in the same season. Smith had 1,563 yards rushing, while Irvin set single-season club records for receptions (93) and receiving

Mr & Mrs T Tailgate with the Pros

Mr & Mrs T is scouting YOU for the Tailgating Association of America.™

yardage (1,523). Both players were named to the NFC Pro Bowl squad, along with tight end Jay Novacek and quarterback Troy Aikman. The Cowboys sent four offensive players to the Pro Bowl for the first time since 1979, and Irvin was named the MVP of the Pro Bowl Game.

1992

JONES NAMED TO COMPETITION COMMITTEE - On May 1, Jerry Jones, was appointed to the NFL's Competition Committee by Commissioner Paul Tagliabue. Jones became the first owner to serve on the prestigious committee since the death of Cincinnati's Paul Brown.

FOURTEENTH DIVISION CHAMPIONSHIP - Before a national television audience on ABC's Monday Night Football, the Cowboys defeated the Atlanta Falcons (41-17) at the Georgia Dome to claim the NFC Eastern Division Championship. The victory marked the Cowboys' first divisional title since 1985.

RECORD NUMBER OF OFFENSIVE PRO BOWL SELECTIONS - Six players from the Cowboys offense were selected to play in the Pro Bowl: RB Emmitt Smith, TE Jay Novacek, QB Troy Aikman, WR Michael Irvin, G Nate Newton and C Mark Stepnoski. The six players establish a Dallas Cowboys' record for most offensive players selected to the Pro Bowl.

CLUB RECORD FOR VICTORIES/SMITH EARNS SECOND RUSHING TITLE - On Dec. 27, Dallas defeated Chicago by a 17-14 score at Texas Stadium. The victory was the 13th of the year for Dallas, establishing a new club record for victories in a season. In the Bears game, Emmitt Smith finished the season with 1,713 rushing yards, enabling Smith to become the first player to win back-to-back NFL rushing titles since Eric Dickerson (1983-84).

ROAD ATTENDANCE RECORD SET - The Cowboys set a new team record for road attendance by averaging 72,523 fans per road game in 1992. The team also played before a sold-out stadium in all 16 regular season games for the first time since the 1981 season.

SIXTH NFC TITLE - On January 17, 1993, the Cowboys defeated the San Francisco 49ers by a 30-20 score at Candlestick Park. The victory sends Dallas to Super Bowl XXVII in Pasadena, marking the Cowboys first NFC title, and Super Bowl trip, since 1978.

THIRD WORLD CHAMPIONSHIP - While making an NFL record sixth Super Bowl appearance, the Cowboys defeated Buffalo 52-17 in Super Bowl XXVII at the Rose Bowl in Pasadena on Jan. 31, 1993. The victory enabled the Cowboys to become the only franchise in NFL history to win more than one Super Bowl under two different ownerships. The Super Bowl crowd of 98,374 was the largest crowd to ever witness a Dallas Cowboys game. The game was also wit-

nessed by 133.4 million television viewers, making Super Bowl XXVII the most watched event in television history.

1993

WHITE HOUSE VISIT - The Super Bowl Champion Dallas Cowboys became the first athletic team to visit the White House under the Clinton administration. The Cowboys team visit to the White House was the first in club history. (March 5).

LANDRY HONORED - Former Head Coach Tom Landry, who led Dallas to two Super Bowl wins and five NFC titles in his 29 years at the Cowboys helm, became the eighth member of the Ring of Honor during halftime ceremonies of the Cowboys-N.Y. Giants game on Nov. 7.

RECORD NUMBER OF PRO BOWL SELECTIONS - A NFC-record 11 Dallas players are selected to the Pro Bowl. That group includes a club-record eight offensive selections (seven Pro Bowl starters).

FIFTEENTH DIVISION CHAMPIONSHIP - In the final game of the regular season, the Cowboys defeat the New York Giants 16-13 in overtime at Giants Stadium to claim their 15th division crown and their second consecutive NFC East title. (Jan. 2)

SMITH EARNS THIRD RUSHING TITLE - Emmitt Smith finishes the season with 1,486 yards to earn his third straight NFL rushing crown. He becomes just the fourth man in NFL history to win three consecutive rushing titles.

SEVENTH NFC TITLE - Dallas defeats San Francisco 38-21 in the NFC Championship Game at Texas Stadium. The victory gives the Cowboys a NFL-record seventh conference championship in the first conference title game to be played at Texas Stadium since Jan. 1, 1978 (a 23-6 win over Minnesota).

FOURTH WORLD CHAMPIONSHIP - Dallas becomes one of just three NFL teams to win four Super Bowls by defeating Buffalo (30-13) in Super Bowl XXVIII. The game, played at the Georgia Dome in Atlanta, featured two rushing touchdowns by Super Bowl MVP Emmitt Smith.

1994

SWITZER NAMED HEAD COACH - Barry Switzer is named the new head coach of the Dallas Cowboys—and the third head coach in team history on March 30. Switzer replaces Jimmy Johnson, who stepped down as the Cowboys' head coach the previous day.

DORSETT AND WHITE ENTER HALL OF FAME - Tony Dorsett, the Cowboys all-time leading rusher in his 11-year career with the Cowboys from 1977-87, and Randy White, a nine-time Pro Bowl

You can always tell who has Cowboys Checking.

Serious fan? Get Cowboys Checking, part of Cowboys Banking, only from Bank One. It's a package
of great banking products and cool Cowboys stuff including exclusively designed checks, checkbook cover,
limited edition cap, and lots more. Sign up today. Call or visit any participating Bank One location.

Official Bank of the Dallas Cowboys

1-888-994-5626
Or visit us at www.bankone.com

SIXTEENTH DIVISION CHAMPIONSHIP - The Cowboys clinched the NFC Eastern Division Crown in the first week of December with a 31-19 victory over the Eagles in Philadelphia (Dec. 4).

RECORD NUMBER OF PRO BOWL SELECTIONS - AGAIN — For the second straight year, the Cowboys send 11 players to the Pro Bowl, tying the NFC record that Dallas established in 1993.

NFL RECORD FOR TITLE GAME APPEARANCES - While making a NFL record 13th NFC Championship Game appearance, the Cowboys become the only team in NFL history to advance to at least two championship games in every decade of the team's existence. Dallas fell short of its third straight Super Bowl with a 38-28 loss to the San Francisco 49ers at Candlestick Park on Jan. 15, 1995.

1995

SEVENTEENTH DIVISION CHAMPIONSHIP On Dec. 24, Dallas wrapped up its fourth straight NFC Eastern Division title - a feat that no other NFC East team has accomplished other than the Cowboys teams from 1976 to 1979.

SMITH WINS FOURTH RUSHING CROWN - Emmitt Smith closes the season with a team-record 1,773 rushing yards and a NFL record 25 touchdowns. Smith led the NFL in rushing for the fourth time in five years, becoming just the fifth player in NFL history to win at least four rushing titles.

TEN PRO BOWLERS SELECTED - Ten Cowboys are selected to the NFC Pro Bowl squad. Since 1993, Dallas has earned 32 Pro Bowl selections - the most ever by one team over a three-year period of time.

EIGHTH NFC TITLE - The Cowboys win a NFL record eighth conference championship game by defeating the Green Bay Packers 38-27 at Texas Stadium on Jan. 14, 1996. The victory marked the Cowboys third NFC title in four years and ensured the team of a NFL record eighth Super Bowl appearance.

THREE SUPER BOWL TITLES IN FOUR YEARS - Dallas becomes the first team in NFL history to win three Super Bowls in a four year period by defeating the Pittsburgh Steelers 27-17 in Super Bowl XXX at Sun Devil Stadium in Tempe, AZ. The game, played on Jan. 28, 1996, is witnessed by 138.4 million television viewers, making Super Bowl XXX the most watched event in television history. The victory enables Dallas to earn its fifth Super Bowl title - joining the San Francisco 49ers as the only NFL franchises to win five Super Bowls. The Cowboys have now appeared in a NFL record eight Super Bowls - three more than any other team.

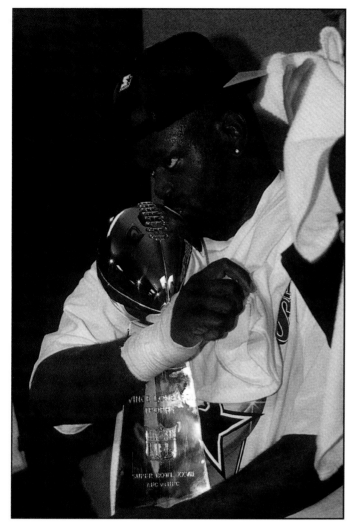

Super Bowl XXVIII MVP Emmitt Smith and the Cowboys second straight Lombardi Trophy.

defensive tackle in his 14-year career with the Cowboys from 1975-88, are both inducted into the Pro Football Hall of Fame in their first year of eligibility. Enshrined on July 30 at Canton, Ohio, both men join former Dallas players Bob Lilly and Roger Staubach as well as Tom Landry and Tex Schramm in the Hall of Fame.

NFL RECORD CROWD IN MEXICO CITY - The Cowboys travel to Mexico City to play the Houston Oilers in a preseason game in front of 112,376 fans, the largest crowd to ever witness a NFL game (Aug. 15).

DORSETT AND WHITE HONORED - Former All-Pros, running back Tony Dorsett and defensive tackle Randy White, became the ninth and tenth members of the Ring of Honor. They were honored during ceremonies at halftime of the Arizona Cardinals game on Oct. 9.

HYUNDAI

CHECK OUT THE NEW LINE-UP FROM HYUNDAI. BETTER CARS. IMPROVED STYLING. AND A RENEWED COMMITMENT TO QUALITY. IN FACT, EVERY HYUNDAI CARRIES ONE OF THE MOST COMPREHENSIVE WARRANTY PACKAGES IN THE INDUSTRY, INCLUDING THREE-YEAR/36,000 MILE ROADSIDE ASSISTANCE. WHICH MEANS NOW ALL YOU HAVE TO WORRY ABOUT IS GRABBING A HOTDOG BEFORE KICKOFF. QUALITY AND COMMITMENT. IT REALLY IS A WHOLE NEW HYUNDAI. **SEE THE ENTIRE LINE AT YOUR NEARBY HYUNDAI DEALER TODAY.** CALL 1·800·826·CARS OR VISIT OUR WEBSITE AT WWW.HYUNDAIUSA.COM.

Elantra Wagon

Elantra

Accent

Sonata

Tiburon

DRIVING IS BELIEVING

DALLAS/DENTON/FT. WORTH
AREA HYUNDAI DEALERS

Allen Samules Hyundai
7740 NE Loop 820
Ft. Worth, TX 76180
817-284-2184

Eckert Hyundai, Inc.
3811 South I-35 E.
Denton, TX 76205
940-382-7777

Hilcher Hyundai
1400 West I-20
Arlington, TX 76017
817-467-3673

Big Billy Barrett Hyundai
16200 LBJ Freeway
Mesquite, TX 75150
972-270-2080

Davis Hyundai
39690 LBJ Freeway S.
Dallas, TX 76376
972-709-2000

Freeman Hyundai
1800 East Airport Freeway
Irving, TX 75062
972-438-2121

Huffines Hyundai
909 Coit Road
Plano, TX 75093
972-867-5000

West Loop Hyundai
3300 Alta Mere
Ft. Worth, TX 76116
817-244-3070

DRIVING IS BELIEVING

New England vs. Denver, Nov. 28, 1976
Oakland vs. Green Bay, Sept. 17, 1978
Buffalo vs. Washington, Nov. 3, 1996

Fewest First Downs, Rushing, Game
0   By many teams. Last time: Washington vs. N.Y. Giants, Dec. 13, 1997

Most First Downs, Rushing, Both Teams, Game
36   Philadelphia (25) vs. Washington (11), Dec. 2, 1951
31   Detroit (18) vs. Washington (13), Sept. 30, 1951
30   Los Angeles (17) vs. Minnesota (13), Nov. 5, 1961
      New Orleans (17) vs. Green Bay (13), Sept. 9, 1979
      New Orleans (16) vs. San Francisco (14), Nov. 11, 1979
      New England (16) vs. Kansas City (14), Oct. 4, 1981

Fewest First Downs, Rushing, Both Teams, Game
2   Houston (0) vs. Denver (2), Dec. 2, 1962
    N.Y. Jets, (1) vs. St. Louis (1), Dec. 3, 1995
3   Philadelphia (1) vs. Pittsburgh (2), Oct. 27, 1957
    Boston (1) vs. Buffalo (2), Nov. 15, 1964
    Los Angeles (0) vs. San Francisco (3), Dec. 6, 1964
    Pittsburgh (1) vs. St. Louis (2), Nov. 13, 1966
    Seattle (1) vs. New Orleans (2), Sept. 1, 1991
    New Orleans (0) vs. N.Y. Jets (3), Dec. 24, 1995
    Philadelphia (1) vs. Carolina (2), Oct. 27, 1996
    San Diego (1) vs. New Orleans (2), Sept. 7, 1997
4   In many games

Most First Downs, Passing, Season
259   San Diego, 1985
251   Houston, 1990
250   Miami, 1986

Fewest First Downs, Passing, Season
18   Pittsburgh, 1941
23   Brooklyn, 1942
    N.Y. Giants, 1944
24   N.Y. Giants, 1943

Most First Downs, Passing, Game
29   N.Y. Giants vs. Cincinnati, Oct. 13, 1985
27   San Diego vs. Seattle, Sept. 15, 1985
26   Miami vs. Cleveland, Dec. 12, 1988

Fewest First Downs, Passing, Game
0   By many teams. Last time:
    Houston vs. Kansas City, Oct. 9, 1988

Most First Downs, Passing, Both Teams, Game
43   San Diego (23) vs. Cincinnati (20), Dec. 20, 1982
    Miami (24) vs. N.Y. Jets (19), Sept. 21, 1986 (OT)
42   San Francisco (22) vs. San Diego (20), Dec. 11, 1982
41   San Diego (27) vs. Seattle (14), Sept. 15, 1985
    Miami (26) vs. Cleveland (15), Dec. 12, 1988

Fewest First Downs, Passing, Both Teams, Game
0   Brooklyn vs. Pittsburgh, Nov. 29, 1942
1   Green Bay (0) vs. Cleveland (1), Sept. 21, 1941
    Pittsburgh (0) vs. Brooklyn (1), Oct. 11, 1942
    N.Y. Giants (0) vs. Detroit (1), Nov. 7, 1943
    Pittsburgh (0) vs. Chi. Cardinals (1), Nov. 11, 1945
    N.Y. Bulldogs (0) vs. Philadelphia (1), Sept. 22, 1949
    Chicago (0) vs. Buffalo (1), Oct. 7, 1979
2   In many games

Most First Downs, Penalty, Season
43   Denver, 1994
42   Chicago, 1987
41   Denver, 1986

Fewest First Downs, Penalty, Season
2   Brooklyn, 1940
4   Chi. Cardinals, 1940
    N.Y. Giants, 1942, 1944
    Washington, 1944
    Cleveland, 1952
    Kansas City, 1969
5   Brooklyn, 1939
    Chi. Bears, 1939
    Detroit, 1953
    Los Angeles, 1953
    Houston, 1982

Most First Downs, Penalty, Game
11   Denver vs. Houston, Oct. 6, 1985
9   Chi. Bears vs. Cleveland, Nov. 25, 1951
    Baltimore vs. Pittsburgh, Oct. 30, 1977
    N.Y. Jets vs. Houston, Sept. 18, 1988
8   Philadelphia vs. Detroit, Dec. 2, 1979
    Cincinnati vs. N.Y. Jets, Oct. 6, 1985
    Buffalo vs. Houston, Sept. 20, 1987
    Houston vs. Atlanta, Sept. 9, 1990
    Kansas City vs. L.A. Raiders, Oct. 3, 1993

Most First Downs, Penalty, Both Teams, Game
11   Chi. Bears (9) vs. Cleveland (2), Nov. 25, 1951
    Cincinnati (8) vs. N.Y. Jets (3), Oct. 6, 1985
    Denver (11) vs. Houston (0), Oct. 6, 1985
    Detroit (6) vs. Dallas (5), Nov. 8, 1987

Continued from page 98

N.Y. Jets (9) vs. Houston (2), Sept. 18, 1988
Kansas City (8) vs. L.A. Raiders (3), Oct. 3, 1993
Detroit (6) vs. San Diego (5), Nov. 11, 1996
10   In many games

Net Yards Gained Rushing and Passing

Most Seasons Leading League
12   Chi. Bears, 1932, 1934-35, 1939, 1941-44, 1947, 1949, 1955-56
7   San Diego, 1963, 1965, 1980-83, 1985
6   L.A. Rams, 1946, 1950-51, 1954, 1957, 1973
    Baltimore, 1958-60, 1964, 1967, 1976
    Dall. Cowboys, 1966, 1968-69, 1971, 1974, 1977

Most Consecutive Seasons Leading League
4   Chi. Bears, 1941-44
    San Diego, 1980-83
3   Baltimore, 1958-60
    Houston, 1960-62
    Oakland, 1968-70
2   By many teams

Most Yards Gained, Season
6,936   Miami, 1984
6,744   San Diego, 1981
6,535   San Diego, 1985

Fewest Yards Gained, Season
1,150   Cincinnati, 1933
1,443   Chi. Cardinals, 1934
1,486   Chi. Cardinals, 1933

Most Yards Gained, Game
735   Los Angeles vs. N.Y. Yanks, Sept. 28, 1951
683   Pittsburgh vs. Chi. Cardinals, Dec. 13, 1958
682   Chi. Bears vs. N.Y. Giants, Nov. 14, 1943

Fewest Yards Gained, Game
−7   Seattle vs. Los Angeles, Nov. 4, 1979
−5   Denver vs. Oakland, Sept. 10, 1967
14   Chi. Cardinals vs. Detroit, Sept. 15, 1940

Most Yards Gained, Both Teams, Game
1,133   Los Angeles (636) vs. N.Y. Yanks (497), Nov. 19, 1950
1,102   San Diego (661) vs. Cincinnati (441), Dec. 20, 1982
1,087   St. Louis (589) vs. Philadelphia (498), Dec. 16, 1962

Fewest Yards Gained, Both Teams, Game
30   Chi. Cardinals (14) vs. Detroit (16), Sept. 15, 1940
136   Chi. Cardinals (50) vs. Green Bay (86), Nov. 18, 1934
154   N.Y. Giants (51) vs. Washington (103), Dec. 11, 1960

Most Consecutive Games, 400 or More Yards Gained
11   San Diego, 1982-83
6   Houston, 1961-62
    San Diego, 1981
    San Francisco, 1987
5   Chi. Bears, 1947
    Philadelphia, 1953
    Chi. Bears, 1955
    Oakland, 1968
    New England, 1981
    Cincinnati, 1986
    San Francisco, 1994

Most Consecutive Games, 300 or More Yards Gained
29   Los Angeles, 1949-51
26   Miami, 1983-85
25   Miami, 1993-95

Rushing

Most Seasons Leading League
16   Chi. Bears, 1932, 1934-35, 1939-42, 1951, 1955-56, 1968, 1977, 1983-86
7   Buffalo, 1962, 1964, 1973, 1975, 1982, 1991-92
6   Cleveland, 1958-59, 1963, 1965-67

Most Consecutive Seasons Leading League
4   Chi. Bears, 1939-42
    Chi. Bears, 1983-86
3   Detroit, 1936-38
    San Francisco, 1952-54
    Cleveland, 1965-67
2   By many teams

Attempts

Most Rushing Attempts, Season
681   Oakland, 1977
674   Chicago, 1984
671   New England, 1978

Fewest Rushing Attempts, Season
211   Philadelphia, 1982
219   San Francisco, 1982
225   Houston, 1982

Most Rushing Attempts, Game
72   Chi. Bears vs. Brooklyn, Oct. 20, 1935
70   Chi. Cardinals vs. Green Bay, Dec. 5, 1948

The day she introduced him to

Cotton Flex™ Khakis

is the day he discovered

Outrageous Comfort.™

Introducing Cotton Flex Khakis. The only 100% cotton khakis that stretch and move as he moves.
Proud sponsor of the Dallas Cowboys.

69 Chi. Cardinals vs. Green Bay, Dec. 6, 1936
Kansas City vs. Cincinnati, Sept. 3, 1978
Fewest Rushing Attempts, Game
6 Chi. Cardinals vs. Boston, Oct. 29, 1933
7 Oakland vs. Buffalo, Oct. 15, 1963
Houston vs. N.Y. Giants, Dec. 8, 1985
Seattle vs. L.A. Raiders, Nov. 17, 1991
Green Bay vs. Miami, Sept. 11, 1994
8 Denver vs. Oakland, Dec. 17, 1960
Buffalo vs. St. Louis, Sept. 9, 1984
Detroit vs. San Francisco, Oct. 20, 1991
Atlanta vs. Detroit, Sept. 5, 1993
Most Rushing Attempts, Both Teams, Game
108 Chi. Cardinals (70) vs. Green Bay (38), Dec. 5, 1948
105 Oakland (62) vs. Atlanta (43), Nov. 30, 1975 (OT)
104 Chi. Bears (64) vs. Pittsburgh (40), Oct. 18, 1936
Fewest Rushing Attempts, Both Teams, Game
34 Atlanta (12) vs. Houston (22), Dec. 5, 1993
Atlanta (15) vs. San Francisco (19), Dec. 24, 1995
35 Seattle (15) vs. New Orleans (20), Sept. 1, 1991
36 Houston (15) vs. N.Y. Jets (21), Oct. 13, 1991

Yards Gained
Most Yards Gained Rushing, Season
3,165 New England, 1978
3,088 Buffalo, 1973
2,986 Kansas City, 1978
Fewest Yards Gained Rushing, Season
298 Philadelphia, 1940
467 Detroit, 1946
471 Boston, 1944
Most Yards Gained Rushing, Game
426 Detroit vs. Pittsburgh, Nov. 4, 1934
423 N.Y. Giants vs. Baltimore, Nov. 19, 1950
420 Boston vs. N.Y. Giants, Oct. 8, 1933
Fewest Yards Gained Rushing, Game
−53 Detroit vs. Chi. Cardinals, Oct. 17, 1943
−36 Philadelphia vs. Chi. Bears, Nov. 19, 1939
−33 Phil-Pitt vs. Brooklyn, Oct. 2, 1943
Most Yards Gained Rushing, Both Teams, Game
595 Los Angeles (371) vs. N.Y. Yanks (224), Nov. 18, 1951
574 Chi. Bears (396) vs. Pittsburgh (178), Oct. 10, 1934
558 Boston (420) vs. N.Y. Giants (138), Oct. 8, 1933
Fewest Yards Gained Rushing, Both Teams, Game
−15 Detroit (−53) vs. Chi. Cardinals (38), Oct. 17, 1943
4 Detroit (−10) vs. Chi. Cardinals (14), Sept. 15, 1940
62 L.A. Rams (15) vs. San Francisco (47), Dec. 6, 1964

Average Gain
Highest Average Gain, Rushing, Season
5.74 Cleveland, 1963
5.65 San Francisco, 1954
5.56 San Diego, 1963
Lowest Average Gain, Rushing, Season
0.94 Philadelphia, 1940
1.45 Boston, 1944
1.55 Pittsburgh, 1935

Touchdowns
Most Touchdowns, Rushing, Season
36 Green Bay, 1962
33 Pittsburgh, 1976
30 Chi. Bears, 1941
New England, 1978
Washington, 1983
Fewest Touchdowns, Rushing, Season
1 Brooklyn, 1934
2 Chi. Cardinals, 1933
Cincinnati, 1933
Pittsburgh, 1934
Philadelphia, 1935
Philadelphia, 1936
Philadelphia, 1937
Philadelphia, 1938
Pittsburgh, 1940
Philadelphia, 1972
N.Y. Jets, 1995
3 By many teams
Most Touchdowns, Rushing, Game
7 Los Angeles vs. Atlanta, Dec. 4, 1976
6 By many teams
Most Touchdowns, Rushing, Both Teams, Game
8 Los Angeles (6) vs. N.Y. Yanks (2), Nov. 18, 1951
Chi. Bears (5) vs. Green Bay (3), Nov. 6, 1955
Cleveland (6) vs. Los Angeles (2), Nov. 24, 1957
7 In many games

Passing

Attempts
Most Passes Attempted, Season
709 Minnesota, 1981
699 New England, 1994
686 New England, 1995
Fewest Passes Attempted, Season
102 Cincinnati, 1933
106 Boston, 1933
120 Detroit, 1937
Most Passes Attempted, Game
70 New England vs. Minnesota, Nov. 13, 1994
68 Houston vs. Buffalo, Nov 1, 1964
66 Atlanta vs. Detroit, Dec. 24, 1989
Fewest Passes Attempted, Game
0 Green Bay vs. Portsmouth, Oct. 8, 1933
Detroit vs. Cleveland, Sept. 10, 1937
Pittsburgh vs. Brooklyn, Nov. 16, 1941
Pittsburgh vs. Los Angeles, Nov. 13, 1949
Cleveland vs. Philadelphia, Dec. 3, 1950
Most Passes Attempted, Both Teams, Game
112 New England (70) vs. Minnesota (42), Nov. 13, 1994
104 Miami (55) vs. N.Y. Jets (49), Oct. 18, 1987 (OT)
102 San Francisco (57) vs. Atlanta (45), Oct. 6, 1985
Fewest Passes Attempted, Both Teams, Game
4 Chi. Cardinals (1) vs. Detroit (3), Nov. 3, 1935
Detroit (0) vs. Cleveland (4), Sept. 10, 1937
6 Chi. Cardinals (2) vs. Detroit (4), Sept. 15, 1940
8 Brooklyn (2) vs. Philadelphia (6), Oct. 1, 1939

Completions
Most Passes Completed, Season
432 San Francisco, 1995
411 Houston, 1991
409 Minnesota, 1994
Fewest Passes Completed, Season
25 Cincinnati, 1933
33 Boston, 1933
34 Chi. Cardinals, 1934
Detroit, 1934
Most Passes Completed, Game
45 New England vs. Minnesota, Nov. 13, 1994 (OT)
42 N.Y. Jets vs. San Francisco, Sept. 21, 1980
41 Houston vs. Dallas, Nov. 10, 1991 (OT)
Fewest Passes Completed, Game
0 By many teams. Last time: Buffalo vs. N.Y. Jets, Sept. 29, 1974
Most Passes Completed, Both Teams, Game
71 New England (45) vs. Minnesota (26), Nov. 13, 1994
68 San Francisco (37) vs. Atlanta (31), Oct. 6, 1985
66 Cincinnati (40) vs. San Diego (26), Dec. 20, 1982
Fewest Passes Completed, Both Teams, Game
1 Chi. Cardinals (0) vs. Philadelphia (1), Nov. 8, 1936
Detroit (0) vs. Cleveland (1), Sept. 10, 1937
Chi. Cardinals (0) vs. Detroit (1), Sept. 15, 1940
Brooklyn (0) vs. Pittsburgh (1), Nov. 29, 1942
2 Chi. Cardinals (0) vs. Detroit (2), Nov. 3, 1935
Buffalo (0) vs. N.Y. Jets (2), Sept. 29, 1974
Chi. Cardinals (0) vs. Green Bay (2), Nov. 18, 1934
3 In seven games

Yards Gained
Most Seasons Leading League, Passing Yardage
10 San Diego, 1965, 1968, 1971, 1978-83, 1985
8 Chi. Bears, 1932, 1939, 1941, 1943, 1945, 1949, 1954, 1964
Washington, 1938, 1940, 1944, 1947-48, 1967, 1974, 1989
7 Houston, 1960-61, 1963-64, 1990-92
Most Consecutive Seasons Leading League, Passing Yardage
6 San Diego, 1978-83
4 Green Bay, 1934-37
3 Miami, 1986-88
Houston, 1990-92
Most Yards Gained, Passing, Season
5,018 Miami, 1984
4,870 San Diego, 1985
4,805 Houston, 1990
Fewest Yards Gained, Passing, Season
302 Chi. Cardinals, 1934
357 Cincinnati, 1933
459 Boston, 1934
Most Yards Gained, Passing, Game
554 Los Angeles vs. N.Y. Yanks, Sept. 28, 1951
530 Minnesota vs. Baltimore, Sept. 28, 1969
521 Miami vs. N.Y. Jets, Oct. 23, 1988
Fewest Yards Gained, Passing, Game
−53 Denver vs. Oakland, Sept. 10, 1967
−52 Cincinnati vs. Houston, Oct. 31, 1971

–39   Atlanta vs. San Francisco, Oct. 23, 1976

Most Yards Gained, Passing, Both Teams, Game

884   N.Y. Jets (449) vs. Miami (435), Sept. 21, 1986 (OT)
883   San Diego (486) vs. Cincinnati (397), Dec. 20, 1982
874   Miami (456) vs. New England (418), Sept. 4, 1994

Fewest Yards Gained, Passing, Both Teams, Game

–11   Green Bay (–10) vs. Dallas (–1), Oct. 24, 1965
  1   Chi. Cardinals (0) vs. Philadelphia (1), Nov. 8, 1936
  7   Brooklyn (0) vs. Pittsburgh (7), Nov. 29, 1942

Times Sacked

Most Seasons Leading League, Fewest Times Sacked

10   Miami, 1973, 1982-90
 4   San Diego, 1963-64, 1967-68
       San Francisco, 1964-65, 1970-71
       N.Y. Jets, 1965-66, 1968, 1993
 3   Houston, 1961-62, 1978
       St. Louis, 1974-76
       Washington, 1966-67, 1991

Most Consecutive Seasons Leading League, Fewest Times Sacked

 9   Miami, 1982-90
 3   St. Louis, 1974-76
 2   By many teams

Most Times Sacked, Season

104   Philadelphia, 1986
 78   Arizona, 1997
 72   Philadelphia, 1987

Fewest Times Sacked, Season

 7   Miami, 1988
 8   San Francisco, 1970
       St. Louis, 1975
 9   N.Y. Jets, 1966
       Washington, 1991

Most Times Sacked, Game

12   Pittsburgh vs. Dallas, Nov. 20, 1966
       Baltimore vs. St. Louis, Oct. 26, 1980
       Detroit vs. Chicago, Dec. 16, 1984
       Houston vs. Dallas, Sept. 29, 1985
11   St. Louis vs. N.Y. Giants, Nov. 1, 1964
       Los Angeles vs. Baltimore, Nov. 22, 1964
       Denver vs. Buffalo, Dec. 13, 1964
       Green Bay vs. Detroit, Nov. 7, 1965
       Buffalo vs. Oakland, Oct. 15, 1967
       Denver vs. Oakland, Nov. 5, 1967
       Atlanta vs. St. Louis, Nov. 24, 1968
       Detroit vs. Dallas, Oct. 6, 1975
       Philadelphia vs. St. Louis, Dec. 18, 1983
       Cleveland vs. Kansas City, Sept. 30, 1984
       Minnesota vs. Chicago, Oct. 28, 1984
       Atlanta vs. Cleveland, Nov. 18, 1984
       Dallas vs. San Diego, Nov. 16, 1986
       Philadelphia vs. Detroit, Nov. 16, 1986
       Philadelphia vs. L.A. Raiders, Nov. 30, 1986 (OT)
       L.A. Raiders vs. Seattle, Dec. 8, 1986
       N.Y. Jets vs. Dallas, Oct. 4, 1987
       Philadelphia vs. Chicago, Oct. 4, 1987
       Dallas vs. Philadelphia, Sept. 15, 1991
       Cleveland vs. Indianapolis, Sept. 6, 1992
10   By many teams

Most Times Sacked, Both Teams, Game

18   Green Bay (10) vs. San Diego (8), Sept. 24, 1978
17   Buffalo (10) vs. N.Y. Titans (7), Nov. 23, 1961
       Pittsburgh (12) vs. Dallas (5), Nov. 20, 1966
       Atlanta (9) vs. Philadelphia (8), Dec. 16, 1984
       Philadelphia (11) vs. L.A. Raiders (6), Nov. 30, 1986 (OT)
16   Los Angeles (11) vs. Baltimore (5), Nov. 22, 1964
       Buffalo (11) vs. Oakland (5), Oct. 15, 1967

Completion Percentage

Most Seasons Leading League, Completion Percentage

14   San Francisco, 1952, 1957-58, 1965, 1981, 1983, 1987, 1989,
       1992-97
11   Washington, 1937, 1939-40, 1942-45, 1947-48, 1969-70
 7   Green Bay, 1936, 1941, 1961-62, 1964, 1966, 1968

Most Consecutive Seasons Leading League, Completion Percentage

 6   San Francisco, 1992-97
 4   Washington, 1942-45
       Kansas City, 1966-69
       San Francisco, 1992-95
 3   Cleveland, 1953-55

Highest Completion Percentage, Season

70.65   Cincinnati, 1982 (310-219)
70.25   San Francisco, 1994 (511-359)
70.19   San Francisco, 1989 (483-339)

Lowest Completion Percentage, Season

22.9   Philadelphia, 1936 (170-39)

24.5   Cincinnati, 1933 (102-25)
25.0   Pittsburgh, 1941 (168-42)

Touchdowns

Most Touchdowns, Passing, Season

49   Miami, 1984
48   Houston, 1961
46   Miami, 1986

Fewest Touchdowns, Passing, Season

 0   Cincinnati, 1933
       Pittsburgh, 1945
 1   Boston, 1932
       Boston, 1933
       Chi. Cardinals, 1934
       Cincinnati/St. Louis, 1934
       Detroit, 1942
 2   Chi. Cardinals, 1932
       Stapleton, 1932
       Chi. Cardinals, 1935
       Brooklyn, 1936
       Pittsburgh, 1942

Most Touchdowns, Passing, Game

 7   Chi. Bears vs. N.Y. Giants, Nov. 14, 1943
       Philadelphia vs. Washington, Oct. 17, 1954
       Houston vs. N.Y. Titans, Nov. 19, 1961
       Houston vs. N.Y. Titans, Oct. 14, 1962
       N.Y. Giants vs. Washington, Oct. 28, 1962
       Minnesota vs. Baltimore, Sept. 28, 1969
       San Diego vs. Oakland, Nov. 22, 1981
 6   By many teams.

Most Touchdowns, Passing, Both Teams, Game

12   New Orleans (6) vs. St. Louis (6), Nov. 2, 1969
11   N.Y. Giants (7) vs. Washington (4), Oct. 28, 1962
       Oakland (6) vs. Houston (5), Dec. 22, 1963
10   San Diego (5) vs. Seattle (5), Sept. 15, 1985
       Miami (6) vs. N.Y. Jets (4), Sept. 21, 1986 (OT)

Passes Had Intercepted

Most Passes Had Intercepted, Season

48   Houston, 1962
45   Denver, 1961
41   Card-Pitt, 1944

Fewest Passes Had Intercepted, Season

 5   Cleveland, 1960
       Green Bay, 1966
       Kansas City, 1990
       N.Y. Giants, 1990
 6   Green Bay, 1964
       St. Louis, 1982
       Dallas, 1993
 7   Los Angeles, 1969

Most Passes Had Intercepted, Game

 9   Detroit vs. Green Bay, Oct. 24, 1943
       Pittsburgh vs. Philadelphia, Dec. 12, 1965
 8   Green Bay vs. N.Y. Giants, Nov. 21, 1948
       Chi. Cardinals vs. Philadelphia, Sept. 24, 1950
       N.Y. Yanks vs. N.Y. Giants, Dec. 16, 1951
       Denver vs. Houston, Dec. 2, 1962
       Chi. Bears vs. Detroit, Sept. 22, 1968
       Baltimore vs. N.Y. Jets, Sept. 23, 1973
 7   By many teams. Last time:
          Green Bay vs. New Orleans, Sept. 14, 1986

Most Passes Had Intercepted, Both Teams, Game

13   Denver (8) vs. Houston (5), Dec. 2, 1962
11   Philadelphia (7) vs. Boston (4), Nov. 3, 1935
       Boston (6) vs. Pittsburgh (5), Dec. 1, 1935
       Cleveland (7) vs. Green Bay (4), Oct. 30, 1938
       Green Bay (7) vs. Detroit (4), Oct. 20, 1940
       Detroit (7) vs. Chi. Bears (4), Nov. 22, 1942
       Detroit (7) vs. Cleveland (4), Nov. 26, 1944
       Chi. Cardinals (8) vs. Philadelphia (3), Sept. 24, 1950
       Washington (7) vs. N.Y. Giants (4), Dec. 8, 1963
       Pittsburgh (9) vs. Philadelphia (2), Dec 12, 1965
10   In many games

Punting

Most Seasons Leading League (Average Distance)

 6   Washington, 1940-43, 1945, 1958
       Denver, 1962-64, 1966-67, 1982
       Kansas City, 1968, 1971-73, 1979, 1984
 5   L.A. Rams, 1946, 1949, 1955-56, 1994

Most Consecutive Seasons Leading League (Average Distance)

 4   Washington, 1940-43
 3   Cleveland, 1950-52
       Denver, 1962-64
       Kansas City, 1971-73

If only the ref had one.

(actual size)

The Casio® JY-10
sees everything the ref can see.
And everything he can't.

Catch every play and replay when you hand off Casio's handheld color TV.
Brilliant 2.3" screen shows the big picture at home or away. And lets you touch down
at other games, too. The perfect way to kickoff tailgate parties. By Casio,
maker of America's best-selling handheld TVs.

Most Punts, Season
114 Chicago, 1981
113 Boston, 1934
    Brooklyn, 1934
112 Boston, 1935
    N.Y. Giants, 1997

Fewest Punts, Season
23 San Diego, 1982
31 Cincinnati, 1982
32 Chi. Bears, 1941

Most Punts, Game
17 Chi. Bears vs. Green Bay, Oct. 22, 1933
   Cincinnati vs. Pittsburgh, Oct. 22, 1933
16 Cincinnati vs. Portsmouth, Sept. 17, 1933
   Chi. Cardinals vs. Chi. Bears, Nov. 30, 1933
   Chi. Cardinals vs. Detroit, Sept. 15, 1940
15 N.Y. Giants vs. Chi. Bears, Nov. 17, 1935
   Philadelphia vs. N.Y. Giants, Dec. 6, 1987 (OT)

Fewest Punts, Game
0 By many teams. Last time: Tampa Bay vs. Miami, Sept. 21, 1997

Most Punts, Both Teams, Game
31 Chi. Bears (17) vs. Green Bay (14), Oct. 22, 1933
   Cincinnati (17), vs. Pittsburgh (14), Oct. 22, 1933
29 Chi. Cardinals (15) vs. Cincinnati (14), Nov. 12, 1933
   Chi. Cardinals (16) vs. Chi. Bears (13), Nov. 30, 1933
   Chi. Cardinals (16) vs. Detroit (13), Sept. 15, 1940
28 Philadelphia (14) vs. Washington (14), Nov. 5, 1939

Fewest Punts, Both Teams, Game
0 Buffalo vs. San Francisco, Sept. 13, 1992
1 Baltimore (0) vs. Cleveland (1), Nov. 1, 1959
  Dall. Cowboys (0) vs. Cleveland (1), Dec. 3, 1961
  Chicago (0) vs. Detroit (1), Oct. 1, 1972
  San Francisco (0) vs. N.Y. Giants (1), Oct. 15, 1972
  Green Bay (0) vs. Buffalo (1), Dec. 5, 1982
  Miami (0) vs. Buffalo (1), Oct. 12, 1986
  Green Bay (0) vs. Chicago (1), Dec. 17, 1989
2 In many games

Average Yardage
Highest Average Distance, Punting, Season
47.6 Detroit, 1961 (56-2,664)
47.0 Pittsburgh, 1961 (73-3,431)
46.9 Pittsburgh, 1953 (80-3,752)
Lowest Average Distance, Punting, Season
32.7 Card-Pitt, 1944 (60-1,964)
33.8 Cincinnati, 1986 (59-1,996)
33.9 Detroit, 1969 (74-2,510)

Punt Returns
Most Seasons Leading League (Average Return)
9 Detroit, 1943-45, 1951-52, 1962, 1966, 1969, 1991
7 Chi. Cardinals/St. Louis, 1948-49, 1955-56, 1959, 1986-87
6 Green Bay, 1950, 1953-54, 1961, 1972, 1996
Most Consecutive Seasons Leading League (Average Return)
3 Detroit, 1943-45
2 By many teams
Most Punt Returns, Season
71 Pittsburgh, 1976
   Tampa Bay, 1979
   L.A. Raiders, 1985
67 Pittsburgh, 1974
   Los Angeles, 1978
   L.A. Raiders, 1984
65 San Francisco, 1976
Fewest Punt Returns, Season
12 Baltimore, 1981
   San Diego, 1982
14 Los Angeles, 1961
   Philadelphia, 1962
   Baltimore, 1982
15 Houston, 1960
   Washington, 1960
   Oakland, 1961
   N.Y. Giants, 1969
   Philadelphia, 1973
   Kansas City, 1982
Most Punt Returns, Game
12 Philadelphia vs. Cleveland, Dec. 3, 1950
11 Chi. Bears vs. Chi. Cardinals, Oct. 8, 1950
   Washington vs. Tampa Bay, Oct. 9, 1977
10 Philadelphia vs. N.Y. Giants, Nov. 26, 1950
   Philadelphia vs. Tampa Bay, Sept. 18, 1977
   Pittsburgh vs. Buffalo, Dec. 16, 1979
   Washington vs. New Orleans, Dec. 26, 1982
   Philadelphia vs. Seattle, Dec. 13, 1992 (OT)
   New England vs. Pittsburgh, Dec. 5, 1993

Most Punt Returns, Both Teams, Game
17 Philadelphia (12) vs. Cleveland (5), Dec. 3, 1950
16 N.Y. Giants (9) vs. Philadelphia (7), Dec. 12, 1954
   Washington (11) vs. Tampa Bay (5), Oct. 9, 1977
15 Detroit (8) vs. Cleveland (7), Sept. 27, 1942
   Los Angeles (8) vs. Baltimore (7), Nov. 27, 1966
   Pittsburgh (8) vs. Houston (7), Dec. 1, 1974
   Philadelphia (10) vs. Tampa Bay (5), Sept. 18, 1977
   Baltimore (9) vs. Kansas City (6), Sept. 2, 1979
   Washington (10) vs. New Orleans (5), Dec. 26, 1982
   L.A. Raiders (8) vs. Cleveland (7), Nov. 16, 1986

Fair Catches
Most Fair Catches, Season
34 Baltimore, 1971
32 San Diego, 1969
31 Minnesota, 1996
Fewest Fair Catches, Season
0 San Diego, 1975
  New England, 1976
  Tampa Bay, 1976
  Pittsburgh, 1977
  Dallas, 1982
1 Cleveland, 1974
  San Francisco, 1975
  Kansas City, 1976
  St. Louis, 1976
  San Diego, 1976
  L.A. Rams, 1982
  St. Louis, 1982
  Tampa Bay, 1982
2 By many teams
Most Fair Catches, Game
7 Minnesota vs. Dallas, Sept. 25, 1966
  Detroit vs. Chicago, Nov. 21, 1976
  Philadelphia vs. Buffalo, Dec. 27, 1987
6 By many teams

Yards Gained
Most Yards, Punt Returns, Season
875 Green Bay, 1996
785 L.A. Raiders, 1985
781 Chi. Bears, 1948
Fewest Yards, Punt Returns, Season
27 St. Louis, 1965
35 N.Y. Giants, 1965
37 New England, 1972
Most Yards, Punt Returns, Game
231 Detroit vs. San Francisco, Oct. 6, 1963
225 Oakland vs. Buffalo, Sept. 15, 1968
219 Los Angeles vs. Atlanta, Oct. 11, 1981
Fewest Yards, Punt Returns, Game
-28 Washington vs. Dallas, Dec. 11, 1966
-23 N.Y. Giants vs. Buffalo, Oct. 20, 1975
    Pittsburgh vs. Houston, Sept. 20, 1970
-20 New Orleans vs. Pittsburgh, Oct. 20, 1968
Most Yards, Punt Returns, Both Teams, Game
282 Los Angeles (219) vs. Atlanta (63), Oct. 11, 1981
245 Detroit (231) vs. San Francisco (14), Oct. 6, 1963
244 Oakland (225) vs. Buffalo (19), Sept. 15, 1968
Fewest Yards, Punt Returns, Both Teams, Game
-18 Buffalo (-18) vs. Pittsburgh (0), Oct. 29, 1972
-14 Miami (-14) vs. Boston (0), Nov. 30, 1969
-13 N.Y. Giants (-13) vs. Cleveland (0), Nov. 14, 1965

Average Yards Returning Punts
Highest Average, Punt Returns, Season
20.2 Chi. Bears, 1941 (27-546)
19.1 Chi. Cardinals, 1948 (35-669)
18.2 Chi. Cardinals, 1949 (30-546)
Lowest Average, Punt Returns, Season
1.2 St. Louis, 1965 (23-27)
1.5 N.Y. Giants, 1965 (24-35)
1.7 Washington, 1970 (27-45)

Touchdowns Returning Punts
Most Touchdowns, Punt Returns, Season
5 Chi. Cardinals, 1959
4 Chi. Cardinals, 1948
  Detroit, 1951
  N.Y. Giants, 1951
  Denver, 1976
3 Washington, 1941
  Detroit, 1952
  Pittsburgh, 1952
  Houston, 1975

Los Angeles, 1981
Cleveland, 1993
Green Bay, 1996
Denver, 1997
San Diego, 1997

Most Touchdowns, Punt Returns, Game

2   Detroit vs. Los Angeles. Oct. 14, 1951
    Detroit vs. Green Bay, Nov. 22, 1951
    Chi. Cardinals vs. Pittsburgh. Nov. 1, 1959
    Chi. Cardinals vs. N.Y. Giants, Nov. 22, 1959
    N.Y. Titans vs. Denver. Sept. 24, 1961
    Denver vs. Cleveland. Sept. 26, 1976
    Los Angeles vs. Atlanta, Oct. 11, 1981
    St. Louis vs. Tampa Bay. Dec. 21, 1986
    L.A. Rams vs. Atlanta. Dec. 27, 1992
    Cleveland vs. Pittsburgh, Oct. 24, 1993
    San Diego vs. Cincinnati, Nov. 2, 1997
    Denver vs. Carolina, Nov. 9, 1997
    Baltimore vs. Seattle, Dec. 7, 1997

Most Touchdowns, Punt Returns, Both Teams, Game

2   Philadelphia (1) vs. Washington (1), Nov. 9, 1952
    Kansas City (1) vs. Buffalo (1), Sept. 11, 1966
    Baltimore (1) vs. New England (1). Nov. 18, 1979
    L.A. Raiders (1) vs. Philadelphia (1), Nov. 30, 1986 (OT)
    Cincinnati (1) vs. Green Bay (1). Sept. 20, 1992
    (Also see previous record)

Kickoff Returns

Most Seasons Leading League (Average Return)

8   Washington, 1942, 1947, 1962-63, 1973-74, 1981, 1995
6   Chicago Bears, 1943, 1948, 1958, 1966, 1972, 1985
5   N.Y. Giants, 1944, 1946, 1949, 1951, 1953

Most Consecutive Seasons Leading League (Average Return)

3   Denver, 1965-67
2   By many teams

Most Kickoff Returns, Season

88 New Orleans, 1980
87 Atlanta, 1996
86 Minnesota, 1984
    Cincinnati, 1994
    Baltimore, 1996

Fewest Kickoff Returns, Season

17 N.Y. Giants, 1944
20 N.Y. Giants, 1941, 1943
    Chi. Bears, 1942
23 Washington, 1942

Most Kickoff Returns, Game

12 N.Y. Giants vs. Washington, Nov. 27, 1966
10 By many teams

Most Kickoff Returns, Both Teams, Game

19 N.Y. Giants (12) vs. Washington (7), Nov. 27, 1966
18 Houston (10) vs. Oakland (8). Dec. 22, 1963
17 Washington (9) vs. Green Bay (8), Oct. 17, 1983
    San Diego (9) vs. Pittsburgh (8), Dec. 8, 1985
    Detroit (9) vs. Green Bay (8), Nov. 27, 1986
    L.A. Raiders (9) vs. Seattle (8), Dec. 18, 1988
    Oakland (10) vs. Seattle (7). Oct. 26, 1997

Yards Gained

Most Yards, Kickoff Returns, Season

1,973   New Orleans, 1980
1,899   New Orleans, 1996
1,840   New Orleans, 1994

Fewest Yards, Kickoff Returns, Season

282   N.Y. Giants. 1940
381   Green Bay. 1940
424   Chicago, 1963

Most Yards, Kickoff Returns, Game

362   Detroit vs. Los Angeles. Oct. 29, 1950
304   Chi. Bears vs. Green Bay. Nov. 9, 1952
      New Orleans vs. L.A. Rams. Oct. 23, 1994
295   Denver vs. Boston. Oct. 4, 1964

Most Yards, Kickoff Returns, Both Teams, Game

560   Detroit (362) vs. Los Angeles (198), Oct. 29, 1950
501   New Orleans (304) vs. L.A. Rams (197). Oct. 23, 1994
453   Washington (236) vs. Philadelphia (217). Sept. 28, 1947

Average Yardage

Highest Average, Kickoff Returns, Season

29.4   Chicago, 1972 (52-1,528)
28.9   Pittsburgh. 1952 (39-1,128)
28.2   Washington, 1962 (61-1,720)

Lowest Average, Kickoff Returns, Season

14.7   N.Y. Jets. 1993 (46-675)
15.8   N.Y. Giants, 1993 (32-507)
15.9   Tampa Bay. 1993 (58-922)

Touchdowns

Most Touchdowns, Kickoff Returns, Season

4   Green Bay, 1967
    Chicago, 1970
    Detroit, 1994
3   Los Angeles, 1950
    Chi. Cardinals, 1954
    San Francisco, 1963
    Denver, 1966
    Chicago, 1967
    New England, 1977
    L.A. Rams, 1985
2   By many teams

Most Touchdowns, Kickoff Returns, Game

2   Chi. Bears vs. Green Bay, Sept. 22, 1940
    Chi. Bears vs. Green Bay, Nov. 9, 1952
    Philadelphia vs. Dallas, Nov. 6, 1966
    Green Bay vs. Cleveland, Nov. 12, 1967
    L.A. Rams vs. Green Bay, Nov. 24, 1985
    New Orleans vs. L.A. Rams. Oct. 23, 1994

Most Touchdowns, Kickoff Returns, Both Teams, Game

2   Washington (1) vs. Philadelphia (1), Nov. 1, 1942
    Washington (1) vs. Philadelphia (1), Sept. 28, 1947
    Los Angeles (1) vs. Detroit (1). Oct. 29, 1950
    N.Y. Yanks (1) vs. N.Y. Giants (1), Nov. 4, 1951 (consecutive)
    Baltimore (1) vs. Chi. Bears (1), Oct. 4, 1958
    Buffalo (1) vs. Boston (1). Nov. 3, 1962
    Pittsburgh (1) vs. Dallas (1). Oct. 30, 1966
    St. Louis (1) vs. Washington (1), Sept. 23, 1973 (consecutive)
    Atlanta (1) vs. San Francisco (1), Dec. 20, 1987 (consecutive)
    Houston (1) vs. Pittsburgh (1). Dec. 4, 1988
    (Also see previous record)

Fumbles

Most Fumbles, Season

56 Chi. Bears, 1938
    San Francisco, 1978
54 Philadelphia, 1946
51 New England, 1973

Fewest Fumbles, Season

8   Cleveland, 1959
11 Green Bay, 1944
12 Brooklyn, 1934
    Detroit, 1943
    Cincinnati, 1982
    Minnesota, 1982

Most Fumbles, Game

10 Phil-Pitt vs. N.Y. Giants, Oct. 9, 1943
    Detroit vs. Minnesota, Nov. 12, 1967
    Kansas City vs. Houston, Oct. 12, 1969
    San Francisco vs. Detroit. Dec. 17, 1978
9   Philadelphia vs. Green Bay. Oct. 13, 1946
    Kansas City vs. San Diego, Nov. 15, 1964
    N.Y. Giants vs. Buffalo. Oct. 20, 1975
    St. Louis vs. Washington, Oct. 25, 1976
    San Diego vs. Green Bay. Sept. 24, 1978
    Pittsburgh vs. Cincinnati. Oct. 14, 1979
    Cleveland vs. Seattle, Dec. 20, 1981
    Cleveland vs. Pittsburgh. Dec. 23, 1990
    Oakland vs. Seattle. Dec. 22, 1996
8   By many teams

Most Fumbles, Both Teams, Game

14 Washington (8) vs. Pittsburgh (6). Nov. 14, 1937
    Chi. Bears (7) vs. Cleveland (7), Nov. 24, 1940
    St. Louis (8) vs. N.Y. Giants (6), Sept. 17, 1961
    Kansas City (10) vs. Houston (4). Oct. 12, 1969
13 Washington (8) vs. Pittsburgh (5). Nov. 14, 1937
    Philadelphia (7) vs. Boston (6), Dec. 8, 1946
    N.Y. Giants (7) vs. Washington (6), Nov. 5, 1950
    Kansas City (9) vs. San Diego (4), Nov. 15, 1964
    Buffalo (7) vs. Denver (6), Dec. 13, 1964
    N.Y. Jets (7) vs. Houston (6), Sept. 12, 1965
    Houston (8) vs. Pittsburgh (5), Dec. 9, 1973
    St. Louis (9) vs. Washington (4), Oct. 25, 1976
    Cleveland (9) vs. Seattle (4), Dec. 20, 1981
    Green Bay (7) vs. Detroit (6), Oct. 6, 1985
12 In many games

Fumbles Lost

Most Fumbles Lost, Season

36 Chi. Cardinals. 1959
31 Green Bay, 1952
29 Chi. Cardinals, 1946
    Pittsburgh, 1950

Fewest Fumbles Lost, Season

S.S. CATALINA
CHARTERED TOURS

S.S. MINNOW
CHARTERED TOURS

se·lect´ ~v. To choose carefully.

There is only one blended Scotch that is matured in old oak
sherry casks for a smoother, mellower finish. Select accordingly.

3   Philadelphia, 1938
    Minnesota, 1980
4   San Francisco, 1960
    Kansas City, 1982
5   Chi. Cardinals, 1943
    Detroit, 1943
    N.Y. Giants, 1943
    Cleveland, 1959
    Minnesota, 1982
    San Diego, 1993
    Detroit, 1996

Most Fumbles Lost, Game
8   St. Louis vs. Washington, Oct. 25, 1976
    Cleveland vs. Pittsburgh, Dec. 23, 1990
7   Cincinnati vs. Buffalo, Nov. 30, 1969
    Pittsburgh vs. Cincinnati, Oct. 14, 1979
    Cleveland vs. Seattle, Dec. 20, 1981
6   By many teams

Fumbles Recovered
Most Fumbles Recovered, Season, Own and Opponents'
58 Minnesota, 1963 (27 own, 31 opp)
51 Chi. Bears, 1938 (37 own, 14 opp)
    San Francisco, 1978 (24 own, 27 opp)
50 Philadelphia, 1987 (23 own, 27 opp)
Fewest Fumbles Recovered, Season, Own and Opponents'
9   San Francisco, 1982 (5 own, 4 opp)
11 Cincinnati, 1982 (5 own, 6 opp)
12 Washington, 1994 (6 own, 6 opp)
    Arizona, 1997 (7 own, 5 opp)
Most Fumbles Recovered, Game, Own and Opponents'
10 Denver vs. Buffalo, Dec. 13, 1964 (5 own, 5 opp)
    Pittsburgh vs. Houston, Dec. 9, 1973 (5 own, 5 opp)
    Washington vs. St. Louis, Oct. 25, 1976 (2 own, 8 opp)
9   St. Louis vs. N.Y. Giants, Sept. 17, 1961 (6 own, 3 opp)
    Houston vs. Cincinnati, Oct. 27, 1974 (4 own, 5 opp)
    Kansas City vs. Dallas, Nov. 10, 1975 (4 own, 5 opp)
    Green Bay vs. Detroit, Oct. 6, 1985 (5 own, 4 opp)
8   By many teams
Most Own Fumbles Recovered, Season
37 Chi. Bears, 1938
28 Pittsburgh, 1987
27 Philadelphia, 1946
    Minnesota, 1963
Fewest Own Fumbles Recovered, Season
2   Washington, 1958
3   Detroit, 1956
    Cleveland, 1959
    Houston, 1982
4   By many teams
Most Opponents' Fumbles Recovered, Season
31 Minnesota, 1963
29 Cleveland, 1951
28 Green Bay, 1946
    Houston, 1977
    Seattle, 1983
Fewest Opponents' Fumbles Recovered, Season
3   Los Angeles, 1974
    Green Bay, 1995
4   Philadelphia, 1944
    San Francisco, 1982
5   Baltimore, 1982
    Arizona, 1997
Most Opponents' Fumbles Recovered, Game
8   Washington vs. St. Louis, Oct. 25, 1976
    Pittsburgh vs. Cleveland, Dec. 23, 1990
7   Buffalo vs. Cincinnati, Nov. 30, 1969
    Cincinnati vs. Pittsburgh, Oct. 14, 1979
    Seattle vs. Cleveland, Dec. 20, 1981
6   By many teams

Touchdowns
Most Touchdowns, Fumbles Recovered, Season, Own and Opponents'
5   Chi. Bears, 1942 (1 own, 4 opp)
    Los Angeles, 1952 (1 own, 4 opp)
    San Francisco, 1965 (1 own, 4 opp)
    Oakland, 1978 (2 own, 3 opp)
4   Chi. Bears, 1948 (1 own, 3 opp)
    Boston, 1948 (4 opp)
    Denver, 1979 (1 own, 3 opp)
    Atlanta, 1981 (1 own, 3 opp)
    Denver, 1984 (4 opp)
•   St. Louis, 1987 (4 opp)
    Minnesota, 1989 (4 opp)
    Atlanta, 1991 (4 opp)
    Philadelphia, 1995 (4 opp)

3   By many teams
Most Touchdowns, Own Fumbles Recovered, Season
2   Chi. Bears, 1953
    New England, 1973
    Buffalo, 1974
    Denver, 1975
    Oakland, 1978
    Green Bay, 1982
    New Orleans, 1983
    Cleveland, 1986
    Green Bay, 1989
    Miami, 1996
Most Touchdowns, Opponents' Fumbles Recovered, Season
4   Detroit, 1937
    Chi. Bears, 1942
    Boston, 1948
    Los Angeles, 1952
    San Francisco, 1965
    Denver, 1984
    St. Louis, 1987
    Minnesota, 1989
    Atlanta, 1991
    Philadelphia, 1995
3   By many teams
Most Touchdowns, Fumbles Recovered, Game, Own and Opponents'
2   By many teams
Most Touchdowns, Fumbled Recovered, Game, Both Teams, Own and Opponents'
3   Detroit (2) vs. Minnesota (1), Dec. 9, 1962 (2 own, 1 opp)
    Green Bay (2) vs. Dallas (1), Nov. 29, 1964 (3 opp)
    Oakland (2) vs. Buffalo (1), Dec. 24, 1967 (3 opp)
    Oakland (2) vs. Philadelphia (1), Sept. 24, 1995 (3 opp)
Most Touchdowns, Own Fumbles Recovered, Game
2   Miami vs. New England, Sept.1, 1996
Most Touchdowns, Opponents' Fumbles Recovered, Game
2   Detroit vs. Cleveland, Nov. 7, 1937
    Philadelphia vs. N.Y. Giants, Sept. 25, 1938
    Chi. Bears vs. Washington, Nov. 28, 1948
    N.Y. Giants vs. Pittsburgh, Sept. 17, 1950
    Cleveland vs. Dall. Cowboys, Dec. 3, 1961
    Cleveland vs. N.Y. Giants, Oct. 25, 1964
    Green Bay vs. Dallas, Nov. 29, 1964
    San Francisco vs. Detroit, Nov. 14, 1965
    Oakland vs. Buffalo, Dec. 24, 1967
    N.Y. Giants vs. Green Bay, Sept. 19, 1971
    Washington vs. San Diego, Sept. 16, 1973
    New Orleans vs. San Francisco, Oct. 19, 1975
    Cincinnati vs. Pittsburgh, Oct. 14, 1979
    Atlanta vs. Detroit, Oct. 5, 1980
    Kansas City vs. Oakland, Oct. 5, 1980
    New England vs. Baltimore, Nov. 23, 1980
    Denver vs. Green Bay, Oct. 15, 1984
    Miami vs. Kansas City, Oct. 11, 1987
    St. Louis vs. New Orleans, Oct. 11, 1987
    Minnesota vs. Atlanta, Dec. 10, 1989
    Philadelphia vs. Phoenix, Nov. 24, 1991
    Cincinnati vs. Seattle, Sept. 6, 1992
    Oakland vs. Philadelphia, Sept. 24, 1995
    Pittsburgh vs. New England, Dec. 16, 1995
    New England vs. San Diego, Dec.1, 1996
Most Touchdowns, Opponents' Fumbled Recovered, Game, Both Teams
3   Green Bay (2) vs. Dallas (1), Nov. 29, 1964
    Oakland (2) vs. Buffalo (1), Dec. 24, 1967
    Oakland (2) vs. Philadelphia (1), Sept. 24, 1995

Turnovers
(Number of times losing the ball on interceptions and fumbles.)
Most Turnovers, Season
63 San Francisco, 1978
58 Chi. Bears, 1947
    Pittsburgh, 1950
    N.Y. Giants, 1983
57 Green Bay, 1950
    Houston, 1962, 1963
    Pittsburgh, 1965
Fewest Turnovers, Season
12 Kansas City, 1982
14 N.Y. Giants, 1943
    Cleveland, 1959
    N.Y. Giants, 1990
16 San Francisco, 1960
    Cincinnati, 1982
    St. Louis, 1982
    Washington, 1982
Most Turnovers, Game
12 Detroit vs. Chi. Bears, Nov. 22, 1942

3 Washington, 1956-58
    Boston, 1964-66
2 By many teams

Most Seasons Leading League, Most Yards Penalized
15 Chi. Bears, 1935, 1937, 1939-44, 1946-47, 1949, 1951, 1961-62, 1968
12 Oakland/L.A. Raiders, 1963-64, 1968-69, 1975, 1982, 1984, 1991, 1993-94, 1996
6 Buffalo, 1962, 1967, 1970, 1972, 1981, 1983
   Houston, 1961, 1985-86, 1988-90

Most Consecutive Seasons Leading League, Most Yards Penalized
6 Chi. Bears, 1939-44
3 Cleveland, 1976-78
   Houston, 1988-90
2 By many teams

Fewest Yards Penalized, Season
139 Detroit, 1937
146 Philadelphia, 1937
159 Philadelphia, 1936

Most Yards Penalized, Season
1,274 Oakland, 1969
1,266 Oakland, 1996
1,239 Baltimore, 1979

Fewest Yards Penalized, Game
0 By many teams. Last time:
     Buffalo vs. Jacksonville, Dec. 14, 1997
     Carolina vs. Green Bay, Dec. 14, 1997

Most Yards Penalized, Game
209 Cleveland vs. Chi. Bears, Nov. 25, 1951
191 Philadelphia vs. Seattle, Dec. 13, 1992 (OT)
190 Tampa Bay vs. Seattle, Oct. 17, 1976

Fewest Yards Penalized, Both Teams, Game
0 Brooklyn vs. Pittsburgh, Oct. 28, 1934
   Brooklyn vs. Boston, Sept. 28, 1936
   Cleveland vs. Chi. Bears, Oct. 9, 1938
   Pittsburgh vs. Philadelphia, Nov. 10, 1940

Most Yards Penalized, Both Teams, Game
374 Cleveland (209) vs. Chi. Bears (165), Nov. 25, 1951
310 Tampa Bay (190) vs. Seattle (120), Oct. 17, 1976
309 Green Bay (184) vs. Boston (125), Oct. 21, 1945

DEFENSE

Scoring

Most Seasons Leading League, Fewest Points Allowed
11 N.Y. Giants, 1927, 1935, 1938-39, 1941, 1944, 1958-59, 1961, 1990, 1993
9 Chi. Bears, 1932, 1936-37, 1942, 1948, 1963, 1985-86, 1988
7 Cleveland, 1951, 1953-57, 1994
   Green Bay, 1929, 1935, 1947, 1962, 1965-66, 1996

Most Consecutive Seasons Leading League, Fewest Points Allowed
5 Cleveland, 1953-57
3 Buffalo, 1964-66
   Minnesota, 1969-71
2 By many teams

Fewest Points Allowed, Season (Since 1932)
44 Chi. Bears, 1932
54 Brooklyn, 1933
59 Detroit, 1934

Most Points Allowed, Season
533 Baltimore, 1981
501 N.Y. Giants, 1966
487 New Orleans, 1980

Fewest Touchdowns Allowed, Season (Since 1932)
6 Chi. Bears, 1932
   Brooklyn, 1933
7 Detroit, 1934
8 Green Bay, 1932

Most Touchdowns Allowed, Season
68 Baltimore, 1981
66 N.Y. Giants, 1966
63 Baltimore, 1950

First Downs

Fewest First Downs Allowed Season
77 Detroit, 1935
79 Boston, 1935
82 Washington, 1937

Most First Downs Allowed, Season
406 Baltimore, 1981
371 Seattle, 1981
366 Green Bay, 1983

Fewest First Downs Allowed, Rushing, Season
35 Chi. Bears, 1942
40 Green Bay, 1939
41 Brooklyn, 1944

    Chi. Cardinals vs. Philadelphia, Sept. 24, 1950
    Pittsburgh vs. Philadelphia, Dec. 12, 1965
11 San Diego vs. Green Bay, Sept. 24, 1978
10 Washington vs. N.Y. Giants, Dec. 4, 1938
   Pittsburgh vs. Green Bay, Nov. 23, 1941
   Detroit vs. Green Bay, Oct. 24, 1943
   Chi. Cardinals vs. Green Bay, Nov. 10, 1946
   Chi. Cardinals vs. N.Y. Giants, Nov. 2, 1952
   Minnesota vs. Detroit, Dec. 9, 1962
   Houston vs. Oakland, Sept. 7, 1963
   Washington vs. N.Y. Giants, Dec. 8, 1963
   Chicago vs. Detroit, Sept. 22, 1968
   St. Louis vs. Washington, Oct. 25, 1976
   N.Y. Jets vs. New England, Nov. 21, 1976
   San Francisco vs. Dallas, Oct. 12, 1980
   Cleveland vs. Seattle, Dec. 20, 1981
   Detroit vs. Denver, Oct. 7, 1984

Most Turnovers, Both Teams, Game
17 Detroit (12) vs. Chi. Bears (5), Nov. 22, 1942
   Boston (9) vs. Philadelphia (8), Dec. 8, 1946
16 Chi. Cardinals (12) vs. Philadelphia (4), Sept. 24, 1950
   Chi. Cardinals (8) vs. Chi. Bears (8), Dec. 7, 1958
   Minnesota (10) vs. Detroit (6), Dec. 9, 1962
   Houston (9) vs. Kansas City (7), Oct. 12, 1969
15 Philadelphia (8) vs. Chi. Cardinals (7), Oct. 3, 1954
   Denver (9) vs. Houston (6), Dec. 2, 1962
   Washington (10) vs. N.Y. Giants (5), Dec. 8, 1963
   St. Louis (9) vs. Kansas City (6), Oct. 2, 1983

Penalties

Most Seasons Leading League, Fewest Penalties
13 Miami, 1968, 1976-84, 1986, 1990-91
9 Pittsburgh, 1946-47, 1950-52, 1954, 1963, 1965, 1968
7 Boston/New England, 1962, 1964-65, 1973, 1987, 1989, 1993

Most Consecutive Seasons Leading League, Fewest Penalties
9 Miami, 1976-84
3 Pittsburgh, 1950-52
2 By many teams

Most Seasons Leading League, Most Penalties
16 Chi. Bears, 1941-44, 1946-49, 1951, 1959-61, 1963, 1965, 1968, 1976
12 Oakland/L.A. Raiders, 1963, 1966, 1968-69, 1975, 1982, 1984, 1991, 1993-96
7 L.A./St. Louis Rams, 1950, 1952, 1962, 1969, 1978, 1980, 1997

Most Consecutive Seasons Leading League, Most Penalties
4 Chi. Bears, 1941-44, 1946-49
   L.A./Oakland Raiders, 1993-96
3 Chi. Cardinals, 1954-56
   Chi. Bears, 1959-61
   Houston, 1988-90

Fewest Penalties, Season
19 Detroit, 1937
21 Boston, 1935
24 Philadelphia, 1936

Most Penalties, Season
156 L.A. Raiders, 1994
    Oakland, 1996
149 Houston, 1989
148 L.A. Raiders, 1993

Fewest Penalties, Game
0 By many teams. Last time:
    Buffalo vs. Jacksonville, Dec. 14, 1997
    Carolina vs. Green Bay, Dec. 14, 1997

Most Penalties, Game
22 Brooklyn vs. Green Bay, Sept. 17, 1944
   Chi. Bears vs. Philadelphia, Nov. 26, 1944
21 Cleveland vs. Chi. Bears, Nov. 25, 1951
20 Tampa Bay vs. Seattle, Oct. 17, 1976
   Oakland vs. Denver, Dec. 15, 1996

Fewest Penalties, Both Teams, Game
0 Brooklyn vs. Pittsburgh, Oct. 28, 1934
   Brooklyn vs. Boston, Sept. 28, 1936
   Cleveland vs. Chi. Bears, Oct. 9, 1938
   Pittsburgh vs. Philadelphia, Nov. 10, 1940

Most Penalties, Both Teams, Game
37 Cleveland (21) vs. Chi. Bears (16), Nov. 25, 1951
35 Tampa Bay (20) vs. Seattle (15), Oct. 17, 1976
33 Brooklyn (22) vs. Green Bay (11), Sept. 17, 1944

Yards Penalized

Most Seasons Leading League, Fewest Yards Penalized
13 Miami, 1967-68, 1973, 1977-84, 1990-91
10 Boston/Washington, 1935, 1953-54, 1956-58, 1970, 1985, 1995, 1997
7 Pittsburgh, 1946-47, 1950, 1952, 1962, 1965, 1968
   Boston/New England, 1962, 1964-66, 1987, 1989, 1993

Most Consecutive Seasons Leading League, Fewest Yards Penalized
8 Miami, 1977-84

Pound the Road.

WITHOUT HAVING TO HEAR ITS CRIES OF PAIN.

THE NISSAN PATHFINDER

The road will get over it. And with the Nissan® Pathfinder® so will you. The Pathfinder's stylish good looks disguise a rugged "go anywhere, do anything" performer. Capable of taking on some of the toughest roads and handling them with ease. It's all thanks to a sturdy foundation and a wealth of standard features that will cradle you in the lap of luxury no matter where you actually are. Take one for a test drive at your local Nissan Dealer today and hit the ground running.

Nissan Motor Corporation U.S.A. Smart people always read the fine print. And they always wear their seatbelts.

Pathfinder's Monoframe™ construction provides a solid platform for improved handling while minimizing noise and vibration.

Most First Downs Allowed, Rushing, Season
- 179   Detroit, 1985
- 178   New Orleans, 1980
- 175   Seattle, 1981

Fewest First Downs Allowed, Passing, Season
- 33   Chi. Bears, 1943
- 34   Pittsburgh, 1941
-      Washington, 1943
- 35   Detroit, 1940
-      Philadelphia, 1940, 1944

Most First Downs Allowed, Passing, Season
- 230   Atlanta, 1995
- 218   San Diego, 1985
- 216   San Diego, 1981
-      N.Y. Jets, 1986

Fewest First Downs Allowed, Penalty, Season
- 1   Boston, 1944
- 3   Philadelphia, 1940
-     Pittsburgh, 1945
-     Washington, 1957
- 4   Cleveland, 1940
-     Green Bay, 1943
-     N.Y. Giants, 1943

Most First Downs Allowed, Penalty, Season
- 48   Houston, 1985
- 46   Houston, 1986
- 43   L.A. Raiders, 1984

Net Yards Allowed Rushing and Passing

Most Seasons Leading League, Fewest Yards Allowed
- 8   Chi. Bears, 1942-43, 1948, 1958, 1963, 1984-86
- 6   N.Y. Giants, 1938, 1940-41, 1951, 1956, 1959
-     Philadelphia, 1944-45, 1949, 1953, 1981, 1991
-     Minnesota, 1969-70, 1975, 1988-89, 1993
- 5   Boston/Washington, 1935-37, 1939, 1946

Most Consecutive Seasons Leading League, Fewest Yards Allowed
- 3   Boston/Washington, 1935-37
-     Chicago, 1984-86
- 2   By many teams

Fewest Yards Allowed, Season
- 1,539   Chi. Cardinals, 1934
- 1,703   Chi. Bears, 1942
- 1,789   Brooklyn, 1933

Most Yards Allowed, Season
- 6,793   Baltimore, 1981
- 6,403   Green Bay, 1983
- 6,352   Minnesota, 1984

Rushing

Most Seasons Leading League, Fewest Yards Allowed
- 10   Chi. Bears, 1937, 1939, 1942, 1946, 1949, 1963, 1984-85, 1987-88
- 7   Detroit, 1938, 1950, 1952, 1962, 1970, 1980-81
-     Philadelphia, 1944-45, 1947-48, 1953, 1990-91
-     Dallas, 1966-69, 1972, 1978, 1992
- 5   N.Y. Giants, 1940, 1951, 1956, 1959, 1986

Most Consecutive Seasons Leading League, Fewest Yards Allowed
- 4   Dallas, 1966-69
- 2   By many teams

Fewest Yards Allowed, Rushing, Season
- 519   Chi. Bears, 1942
- 558   Philadelphia, 1944
- 762   Pittsburgh, 1982

Most Yards Allowed, Rushing, Season
- 3,228   Buffalo, 1978
- 3,106   New Orleans, 1980
- 3,010   Baltimore, 1978

Fewest Touchdowns Allowed, Rushing, Season
- 2   Detroit, 1934
-     Dallas, 1968
-     Minnesota, 1971
- 3   By many teams

Most Touchdowns Allowed, Rushing, Season
- 36   Oakland, 1961
- 31   N.Y. Giants, 1980
-     Tampa Bay, 1986
- 30   Baltimore, 1981

Passing

Most Seasons Leading League, Fewest Yards Allowed
- 9   Green Bay, 1947-48, 1962, 1964-68, 1996
- 7   Washington, 1939, 1942, 1945, 1952-53, 1980, 1985
- 6   Chi. Bears, 1938, 1943-44, 1958, 1960, 1963
-     Minnesota, 1969-70, 1972, 1975-76, 1989
-     Pittsburgh, 1941, 1946, 1951, 1955, 1974, 1990
-     Philadelphia, 1934, 1936, 1940, 1949, 1981, 1991

Most Consecutive Seasons Leading League, Fewest Yards Allowed
- 5   Green Bay, 1964-68
- 2   By many teams

Fewest Yards Allowed, Passing, Season
- 545   Philadelphia, 1934
- 558   Portsmouth, 1933
- 585   Chi. Cardinals, 1934

Most Yards Allowed, Passing, Season
- 4,541   Atlanta, 1995
- 4,389   N.Y. Jets, 1986
- 4,311   San Diego, 1981

Fewest Touchdowns Allowed, Passing, Season
- 1   Portsmouth, 1932
-     Philadelphia, 1934
- 2   Brooklyn, 1933
-     Chi. Bears, 1934
- 3   Chi. Bears, 1932
-     Green Bay, 1932
-     Green Bay, 1934
-     Chi. Bears, 1936
-     New York, 1939
-     New York, 1944

Most Touchdowns Allowed, Passing, Season
- 40   Denver, 1963
- 38   St. Louis, 1969
- 37   Washington, 1961
-     Baltimore, 1981

Sacks

Most Seasons Leading League
- 5   Oakland/L.A. Raiders, 1966-68, 1982, 1986
- 4   Boston/New England, 1961, 1963, 1977, 1979
-     Dallas, 1966, 1968-69, 1978
-     Dallas/Kansas City, 1960, 1965, 1969, 1990
- 3   San Francisco, 1967, 1972, 1976
-     L.A. Rams, 1968, 1970, 1988

Most Consecutive Seasons Leading League
- 3   Oakland, 1966-68
- 2   Dallas, 1968-69

Most Sacks, Season
- 72   Chicago, 1984
- 71   Minnesota, 1989
- 70   Chicago, 1987

Fewest Sacks, Season
- 11   Baltimore, 1982
- 12   Buffalo, 1982
- 13   Baltimore, 1981

Most Sacks, Game
- 12   Dallas vs. Pittsburgh, Nov. 20, 1966
-     St. Louis vs. Baltimore, Oct. 26, 1980
-     Chicago vs. Detroit, Dec. 16, 1984
-     Dallas vs. Houston, Sept. 29, 1985
- 11   N.Y. Giants vs. St. Louis, Nov. 1, 1964
-     Baltimore vs. Los Angeles, Nov. 22, 1964
-     Buffalo vs. Denver, Dec. 13, 1964
-     Detroit vs. Green Bay, Nov. 7, 1965
-     Oakland vs. Buffalo, Oct. 15, 1967
-     Oakland vs. Denver, Nov. 5, 1967
-     St. Louis vs. Atlanta, Nov. 24, 1968
-     Dallas vs. Detroit, Oct. 6, 1975
-     St. Louis vs. Philadelphia, Dec. 18, 1983
-     Kansas City vs. Cleveland, Sept. 30, 1984
-     Chicago vs. Minnesota, Oct. 28, 1984
-     Cleveland vs. Atlanta, Nov. 18, 1984
-     Detroit vs. Philadelphia, Nov. 16, 1986
-     San Diego vs. Dallas, Nov. 16, 1986
-     L.A. Raiders vs. Philadelphia, Nov. 30, 1986 (OT)
-     Seattle vs. L.A. Raiders, Dec. 8, 1986
-     Chicago vs. Philadelphia, Oct. 4, 1987
-     Dallas vs. N.Y. Jets, Oct. 4, 1987
-     Indianapolis vs. Cleveland, Sept. 6, 1992
- 10   By many teams

Most Opponents Yards Lost Attempting to Pass, Season
- 666   Oakland, 1967
- 583   Chicago, 1984
- 573   San Francisco, 1976

Fewest Opponents Yards Lost Attempting to Pass, Season
- 72   Jacksonville, 1995
- 75   Green Bay, 1956
- 77   N.Y. Bulldogs, 1949

Interceptions By

Most Seasons Leading League
- 10   N.Y. Giants, 1933, 1937-39, 1944, 1948, 1951, 1954, 1961, 1997
- 8   Green Bay, 1940, 1942-43, 1947, 1955, 1957, 1962, 1965
-     Chi. Bears, 1935-36, 1941-42, 1946, 1963, 1985, 1990

      6 Kansas City, 1966-70, 1974
Most Consecutive Seasons Leading League
      5 Kansas City, 1966-70
      3 N.Y. Giants, 1937-39
      2 By many teams
Most Passes Intercepted By, Season
    49 San Diego, 1961
    42 Green Bay, 1943
    41 N.Y. Giants, 1951
Fewest Passes Intercepted By, Season
      3 Houston, 1982
      5 Baltimore, 1982
      6 Houston, 1972
          St. Louis, 1982
          Atlanta, 1996
Most Passes Intercepted By, Game
      9 Green Bay vs. Detroit, Oct. 24, 1943
          Philadelphia vs. Pittsburgh, Dec. 12, 1965
      8 N.Y. Giants vs. Green Bay, Nov. 21, 1948
          Philadelphia vs. Chi. Cardinals, Sept. 24, 1950
          N.Y. Giants vs. N.Y. Yanks, Dec. 16, 1951
          Houston vs. Denver, Dec. 2, 1962
          Detroit vs. Chicago, Sept. 22, 1968
          N.Y. Jets vs. Baltimore, Sept. 23, 1973
      7 By many teams. Last time:
              New Orleans vs. Green Bay, Sept. 14, 1986
Most Consecutive Games, One or More Interceptions By
    46 L.A. Chargers/San Diego, 1960-63
    37 Detroit, 1960-63
    36 Boston, 1944-47
Most Yards Returning Interceptions, Season
   929 San Diego, 1961
   712 Los Angeles, 1952
   697 Seattle, 1984
Fewest Yards Returning Interceptions, Season
      5 Los Angeles, 1959
    37 Dallas, 1989
    41 Atlanta, 1996
Most Yards Returning Interceptions, Game
   325 Seattle vs. Kansas City, Nov. 4, 1984
   314 Los Angeles vs. San Francisco, Oct. 18, 1964
   245 Houston vs. N.Y. Jets, Oct. 15, 1967
Most Yards Returning Interceptions, Both Teams, Game
   356 Seattle (325) vs. Kansas City (31), Nov. 4, 1984
   338 Los Angeles (314) vs. San Francisco (24), Oct. 18, 1964
   308 Dallas (182) vs. Los Angeles (126), Nov. 2, 1952
Most Touchdowns, Returning Interceptions, Season
      9 San Diego, 1961
      7 Seattle, 1984
      6 Cleveland, 1960
          Green Bay, 1966
          Detroit, 1967
          Houston, 1967
Most Touchdowns Returning Interceptions, Game
      4 Seattle vs. Kansas City, Nov. 4, 1984
      3 Baltimore vs. Green Bay, Nov. 5, 1950
          Cleveland vs. Chicago, Dec. 11, 1960
          Philadelphia vs. Pittsburgh, Dec. 12, 1965
          Baltimore vs. Pittsburgh, Sept. 29, 1968
          Buffalo vs. N.Y. Jets, Sept. 29, 1968
          Houston vs. San Diego, Dec. 19, 1971
          Cincinnati vs. Houston, Dec. 17, 1972
          Tampa Bay vs. New Orleans, Dec. 11, 1977
      2 By many teams
Most Touchdown Returning Interceptions, Both Teams, Game
      4 Philadelphia (3) vs. Pittsburgh (1), Dec. 12, 1965
          Seattle (4) vs. Kansas City (0), Nov. 4, 1984
      3 Los Angeles (2) vs. Detroit (1), Nov. 1, 1953
          Cleveland (2) vs. N.Y. Giants (1), Dec. 18, 1960
          Pittsburgh (2) vs. Cincinnati (1), Oct. 10, 1983
          Kansas City (2) vs. San Diego (1), Oct. 19, 1986
          (Also see previous record)

Punt Returns
Fewest Opponents Punt Returns, Season
      7 Washington, 1962
          San Diego, 1982
    10 Buffalo, 1982
    11 Boston, 1962
Most Opponents Punt Returns, Season
    71 Tampa Bay, 1976, 1977
    69 N.Y. Giants, 1953
    68 Cleveland, 1974
Fewest Yards Allowed, Punt Returns, Season
    22 Green Bay, 1967
    34 Washington, 1962

    39 Cleveland, 1959
          Washington, 1972
Most Yards Allowed, Punt Returns, Season
   932 Green Bay, 1949
   913 Boston, 1947
   906 New Orleans, 1974
Lowest Average Allowed, Punt Returns, Season
  1.20 Chi. Cardinals, 1954 (46-55)
  1.22 Cleveland, 1959 (32-39)
  1.55 Chi. Cardinals, 1953 (44-68)
Highest Average Allowed, Punt Returns, Season
  18.6 Green Bay, 1949 (50-932)
  18.0 Cleveland, 1977 (31-558)
  17.9 Boston, 1960 (20-357)
Most Touchdowns Allowed, Punt Returns, Season
      4 New York, 1959
          Atlanta, 1992
      3 Green Bay, 1949
          Chi. Cardinals, 1951
          L.A. Rams, 1951, 1994
          Washington, 1952
          Dallas, 1952
          Pittsburgh, 1959, 1993
          N.Y. Jets, 1968
          Cleveland, 1977
          Atlanta, 1986
          Tampa Bay, 1986
      2 By many teams

Kickoff Returns
Fewest Opponents Kickoff Returns, Season
    10 Brooklyn, 1943
    13 Denver, 1992
    15 Detroit, 1942, Brooklyn, 1944
Most Opponents Kickoff Returns, Season
    91 Washington, 1983
    89 New England, 1980, San Francisco, 1994, Denver, 1997
    88 San Diego, 1981, Pittsburgh, 1995
Fewest Yards Allowed, Kickoff Returns, Season
   225 Brooklyn, 1943
   254 Denver, 1992
   293 Brooklyn, 1944
Most Yards Allowed, Kickoff Returns, Season
 2,045 Kansas City, 1966
 1,912 San Francisco, 1994
 1,857 San Francisco, 1995
Lowest Average Allowed, Kickoff Returns, Season
  14.3 Cleveland, 1980 (71-1,018)
  14.9 Indianapolis, 1993 (37-551)
  15.0 Seattle, 1982 (24-361)
Highest Average Allowed, Kickoff Returns, Season
  29.5 N.Y. Jets, 1972 (47-1,386)
  29.4 Los Angeles, 1950 (48-1,411)
  29.1 New England, 1971 (49-1,427)
Most Touchdowns Allowed, Kickoff Returns, Season
      3 Minnesota, 1963, 1970, Dallas, 1966, Detroit, 1980, Pittsburgh, 1986, Buffalo, 1997
      2 By many teams

Fumbles
Fewest Opponents Fumbles, Season
    11 Cleveland, 1956, Baltimore, 1982
    12 Green Bay, 1995
    13 Los Angeles, 1956, Chicago 1960, Cleveland, 1963, Cleveland, 1965, Detroit, 1967' San Diego, 1969
Most Opponents Fumbles, Season
    50 Minnesota, 1963, San Francisco, 1978
    48 N.Y. Giants, 1980, N.Y. Jets, 1986
    47 N.Y. Giants, 1977, Seattle, 1984

PREVENT DEFENSE

BACKFIELD IN MOTION

BLITZ

The Dallas Cowboys Cheerleaders recently reached a major milestone in the entertainment industry by making more international entertainment trips to U.S. military bases than any other professional performer or group over the past ten years. An American institution that is recognized worldwide, the Cheerleaders are currently in their third decade of operation at Texas Stadium. The Cowboys transformed the idea of sideline cheerleaders in 1972 when they mixed a unique blend of glamour and dance with an old football tradition. Nobody at the time predicted the Dallas Cowboys Cheerleaders would become an international phenomenon, but that's precisely what happened.

The image and style of the Cowboys Cheerleaders has had an enormous influence on entertainment in sports. But while the Cowboys Cheerleaders have been imitated throughout the sports world, no one has been able to equal their stature.

The strength of their national popularity was evident during the 1970's when two made-for-TV movies about the Cowboys Cheerleaders drew top ratings. That popularity has grown in the 1990's with an annual ESPN Swimsuit Special and an appearance on Saturday Night Live.

Besides being an integral part of Cowboys games at Texas Stadium, the Cheerleaders perform at numerous state fairs, college halftime shows and other events around the country.

The Cowboys Cheerleaders also donate their time to many charitable and civic causes. Every year, the Cheerleaders visit hospitals, nursing homes and schools. They perform at telethons and other fund-raising events around the United States. And they bring their special brand of goodwill to American military bases in places like Korea, the Philippines, Cuba, Panama, Italy, the Indian Ocean and the Persian Gulf.

The Cowboys Cheerleaders' annual USO/ Department of Defense tours every Christmas and spring have become a special tradition. Since 1979, the Cheerleaders have visited and entertained hundreds of thousands of United States military personnel all over the world on 36 USO/DOD tours. In 1997, the squad received the first-ever "Spirit of Hope" Award from the USO in recognition of distinguished service to American Troops stationed overseas.

The Cheerleaders are under the direction of Kelli McGonagill Finglass and choreographed by Judy Trammell.

Camp DCC

Each summer, the Dallas Cowboys Cheerleaders offer a selection of day camps for girls ages seven and up. This provides campers an opportunity to work with, and learn from, the most renowned cheerleading squad ever. Participants are grouped by age and learn warm-ups, cheers, chants, dance routines, jumps and kicklines. Camp DCC is a fun learning and development program focused on improving the talents and abilities of each individual participant in a non-competitive environment. For more information, call the Dallas Cowboys Cheerleaders at 972/556-9932.

Hey, Jerry.

You could've gotten the guaranteed low price on our sanders.

Proud sponsor of the Dallas Cowboys.

When the Dallas Cowboys open their 39th training camp this summer, the new site will be Midwestern State University in Wichita Falls, Texas. As part of the team's commitment to keeping their training camp in Texas, the Cowboys selected Midwestern State University as the new home of the Cowboys preseason preparations. This will mark the ninth consecutive year the Cowboys have held camp in Texas.

The camp at Midwestern State offers a rare opportunity for Cowboys' fans from all over the state of Texas and the Southwest to get an "up close and personal look" at their favorite team.

Upon purchasing the team in 1989, Cowboys' President and General Manager Jerry Jones was determined to bring the team back to Texas and its fans at home. By moving the team first to Austin and now to Wichita Falls, Jones has cited the moves as a means of "bringing the state's Cowboys fans closer to their team. As we see it," Jones says, "the Dallas Cowboys represent all of Texas, and I saw first hand how much excitement there can be at an in-state train-

ing camp. Our fans throughout the state and the southwest will continue to have that opportunity to become closer with their team in Wichita Falls."

Since the Cowboys moved their training camp to Texas, the team has had six winning seasons, won an unprecedented five consecutive NFC Eastern Division titles, won three Super Bowls and played in four NFC Championship Games. The team has also compiled a composite record of 95-48 for a winning percentage of 66.4% since moving to Texas from Thousand Oaks, Calif. prior to the 1990 season.

With a full slate of events scheduled for 1998, the Cowboys' Wichita Falls based camp will be a special summer attraction to Cowboys fans from around the State of Texas

and the Southwest. With two major highways and flights in and out of DFW Airport daily, Wichita Falls makes for convenient travel. It is just a two-hour drive from Dallas-Ft. Worth and Oklahoma City, making day trips to camp an easy option.

TRAINING CAMP FACTS

WICHITA FALLS has a population of approximately 140,000 people and is the largest city within a 100 mile radius. Located 15 miles south of the Oklahoma border, it is equidistant from Dallas-Ft. Worth and Oklahoma City. Wichita Falls is also home to Sheppard Air Force Base, home of the NATO jet pilot training program and the largest employer in the city.

MIDWESTERN STATE UNIVERSITY is a public university that was founded in 1922 and became part of the Texas Colleges and Universities system in 1961. MSU has 5,800 students in 37 baccalaureate programs and 18 master's programs. The 170-acre campus has state-of-the-art facilities available to the Cowboys, including a new dining hall, a new residence hall and a coliseum which houses two gymnasiums, a pool, weight room and indoor running track.

DATES: Camp this year runs from July 15 through August 15.

PRACTICES: Cowboys practice sessions at Midwestern State are open to the public free of charge. Limited public parking is available on campus during practice times.

INFORMATION: Further information on Cowboys training camp, and training camp sponsorships, can be obtained by calling the Dallas Cowboys Office in Irving at 214/556-9308.

FRONT OFFICE

Jerry Jones............President and General Manager
Stephen Jones.................Executive Vice President/
.................................Director of Player Personnel
Charlotte Anderson............Vice President/ Director
.................................of Marketing and Special Events
Jerry Jones, Jr., ...Vice President/Legal Operations
George Hays.................Vice President of Marketing

COACHING STAFF

Chan Gailey.................................Head Coach
Joe Avezzano.........................Special Teams
Jim Bates......Assistant Head Coach/ Defensive Line
Dave Campo.........................Defensive Coordinator
George Edwards.........................Linebackers
Buddy Geis.................................Quarterbacks
Steve Hoffman.....................Kickers/Quality Control
Hudson Houck.........................Offensive Line
Jim Jeffcoat.........................Defensive Line Assistant
Joe Juraszek.....................Strength and Conditioning
Les Miles.................................Tight Ends
Dwain Painter.........................Wide Receivers
Clancy Pendergast.................Defensive Assistant/
.................................Quality Control
Tommie Robinson.........................Offensive Assistant
Clarence Shelmon.........................Running Backs
Mike Zimmer.........................Defensive Backs
Charlie Biggurs.........................Assistant Strength
.................................and Conditioning
Blake Cundiff.........................Assistant Strength
.................................and Conditioning
Marge Anderson.................Administrative Assistant
Barbara Goodman.................Administrative Assistant

PLAYER PERSONNEL

Stephen Jones.............Director of Player Personnel
Larry Lacewell.....................Director of College
.................................and Pro Scouting
Walter Juliff.....................Assistant Director
.................................of College and Pro Scouting
Tom Ciskowski.................................Scout
Jim Garrett.................................Scout
Jim Hess.................................Scout
Bobby Marks.................................Scout
Walt Yowarsky.................................Scout
Chris Hall.................................Assistant

MARKETING

George Hays.................Vice President of Marketing
Charlotte Anderson.................Director of Marketing
.................................and Special Events
Doreen Bice.................Marketing and Special Events
.................................Coordinator
John Hickman.......Sales and Marketing Coordinator
Donna Sullivan.........................Marketing Assistant
Bridgette Smith.........................Marketing Assistant
Ted Ovletrea.........................Team Mascot

FRONT OFFICE STAFF

Marylyn Love.....................Executive Assistant
.................................to the General Manager
Bruce Mays.........................Director of Operations
Calvin Hill.................................Consultant
Robert Newhouse.........................Director of Player
.................................Assistance and Development
Susan Skaggs.................Director of Civic Affairs
Craig Glieber.........Assistant Director of Operations

Steve Carichoff.........................Operations Assistant
Laura Fryar.........................Administrative Assistant
Connie Medina.................Administrative Assistant
Todd Williams.................................Assistant

PUBLIC RELATIONS

Rich Dalrymple.................Director of Public Relations
Brett Daniels.........................Assistant Director of
.................................Public Relations
Doug Hood.................................Assistant
Rhonda Worthey.......Assistant/Community Relations

TICKET OPERATIONS

Carol Padgett.................Director of Ticket Operations
Ann Bihari....Assistant Director of Ticket Operations
Joy Dotson.................................Assistant
Glinda Galvan.................Ticket Office Representative
Andrea Payne.................Ticket Office Representative
Sandra Williams.........Ticket Office Representative
Casey Yocom.................Ticket Office Representative

VIDEO

Robert Blackwell.................................Director
Mike Maples.................................Assistant
Jim Seeley.................................Intern

MEDICAL

Jim Maurer.................................Head Trainer
Britt Brown.........................Assistant Trainer
Bob Haas.........................Assistant Trainer
Greg Gaither.................................Intern
Dr. Robert Vandermeer.................Team Physician
Dr. Dan Cooper.................Team Physician
Dr. J.R. Zamorano.................Team Physician
Dr. Robert Fowler.................Team Physician

EQUIPMENT

Mike McCord.........................Equipment Manager
Bucky Buchanan.......Assistant Equipment Manager
Louis Jackson.................................Assistant
Hollis Jackson.................................Intern

SALES AND PROMOTIONS

Joel Finglass.................................Director
Travis Clark.................................Assistant Director
Jim Engstrom.................................Assistant Director
Dana Elliott.........................Office Manager
Dale Boutwell.................................Sales
Ronda Cates.................................Sales
Michelle Druga.................................Sales
Dave Handal.................................Sales
Tandra Johnson.................................Sales
Steve Obert.................................Sales
Grady Siske.................................Sales

ACCOUNTING

Robert Nunez.................................Treasurer
Jamé Grazer.................................Controller
Brian England.........................Payroll Manager
Cathy Lowe.........................Assistant Controller
Alicia Cox.................Assistant Accounting Manager
Michael Crouch.......Assistant Accounting Manager
Chris Linehan.................Texas Stadium Assistant
.................................Accounting Manager
Kristi Burnham.........Assistant Accounting Manager

BUILDING OPERATIONS/PRACTICE FIELDS

Steve Forgey.........................Building Engineer
Steve Landers.................................Assistant
Kevin O'Reilly.................................Assistant
Al Walker.................................Assistant
Kathy Coleman.........................Mail Room/Supplies
Jesse Leija.........................Mail Room Assistant
Curtis Manning.................................Security
Bryan Wansley.................................Security

COWBOYS WEEKLY NEWSPAPER

Russ Russell.................................Publisher
Jim Browder.................................Editor
Sharon Carnahan.................Circulation Manager
Cheryl Harris.........................Production Manager
Kay Clark.........................Administrative Assistant
Jonnie Haug.................................Assistant
James Topalian.................................Assistant

COWBOYS TELEVISION PRODUCTION

John Chang.................Director of Television
Scott Purcel.................................Senior Producer
Machelle Webb.....Syndication and Traffic Manager
Brandi Drawe.........................Producer and Reporter
Nahala Johnson.................................Videographer
Jorge Infante.................Producer, Spanish Radio

DALLAS COWBOYS CHEERLEADERS

Charlotte Anderson.................................President
Kelli McGonagill Finglass.................................Director
Judy Trammell.................................Choreographer
Shelly McCaslin.................Assistant Choreographer
Dan Devens.........................Graphic Design
Kandra Hall.........................Administrative Assistant
Rachel Durbin.................................Receptionist

TEXAS STADIUM

Stephen Jones.................................President
Bruce Hardy...Vice President and General Manager
Amy Phillips...Vice President of Food and Beverage
Bill Priakos.................Director of Novelties
Ron Underwood.................Director of Operations
Cynthia Smith.................................Controller
Terri Van Hooser.........................Assistant Controller
Glenn Kimberlin....Administrative Assist./Operations
Becky Elliott.........................Administrative Assistant
Susan Skaggs.................Director of Special Events
David Lavender.................Director of Maintenance
Steve Epperson.................Director of Housekeeping
George Wasai.................Director of Concessions
Jeannie Sprufera.................Director of Suite Services
Michael Mudrone.................................Executive Chef
Nicole Kubitza.................Catering Sales Manager
Barbara Ruggles.................Stadium Club Manager
Wes Harrell.........................Beverage Manager
Roderick Mitchell.................Concessions Manager
Richard Rodriguez.................Purchasing Manager
Jeff Schmidt.........................Telemarketing Manager
Tanya Price.................Suite Services Coordinator
Brad London.................Catering Coordinator
Aric Griffin.................................Sous Chef
Henry Gonzales.................................Chef
Juan Vela.................................Chef
Nemecio Rodriguez.................Banquet Supervisor
Sanko Prioleau.................................Warehouse
Kristi Behlmann.................Concessions Assistant